The LETTERS of OSCAR WENDLOW

London Cabbie and Portrait Painter to the Stars

BOXTREE

Oscar Wendlow
'Portrait Painter To The Stars'
Cleveland Road, Barnes,
London SW13 0AA

15th October 1997

Melvyn Bragg, Esq.,
'Start The Week',
Room 6098,
Broadcasting House,
Portland Place,
London,
W1A 1AA.

Dear Mr. Bragg,

Please allow me to introduce myself. My name is Oscar and I am a licensed black-cab driver of some 22 years, and more recently 'portrait painter to the stars'.

Having been a keen 'Sunday painter' for some time I have recently felt so encouraged by people's compliments on my work that I have decided to MAKE A GO OF IT!! Our children Anthea and Raoul are both young adults now and less dependent on Joyce (my other 'alf) and myself, apart from cash handouts that is! After 22 years of cabbing the mortgage is almost paid off and we have managed to 'put a bit by'. In other words we are COMFORTABLE! Ever since I took up painting some 2 years ago I have dreamed of becoming a full-time ARTIST! Well, a few weeks ago I looked in the mirror and I thought, "It's now or never, Oz", (friends call me Oz for short) (you can call me Oz). At that moment I knew I had to try and make a GO of my painting or forever hold my peace (so to speak).

Cabbies have logical minds so I knew I needed a strategy and it is this: Up to now I have painted friends, members of my family and famous people from photographs. What I now intend to do is concentrate on the famous people but paint them 'in the flesh'. I then plan to show them to the West End galleries with a view to an exhibition called 'British Superstars of the Arts and Culture and Pop Music in Britain at the Rear End of the Nineties'. As you are one of our foremost spokespersons on matters cultural AND a novelist 'to boot' I would very much like to have your portrait in my exhibition!

Would you consider 'sitting' for me at a time and place of your convenience? I reckon about 6 three-hour sessions would suffice. I would be very grateful if you would consider doing me this honour and helping me to 'get things off the ground'.

Incidentally, I am offering all 'sitters' optional 'blemish enhancement', i.e. if somebody has a physical attribute they dislike like sticking-out-ears, I will happily reduce the 'effect' in my portrait. Forgive me for being personal but you do appear to have a broken nose. If you like I could give you a normal, thin nose (or any nose of your choice!) in my painting. That is something we could discuss at a later date.

I do hope you will respond favourably to my request and I look forward to hearing from you.

Yours sincerely,

Oscar Wendlow

Life without art would be like eating a packet of salt and vinegar crisps with just the salt on them and no vinegar on.

Oscar Wendlow 1999

First published in 1999 by Boxtree, an imprint of Macmillan Publishers Ltd, 25 Eccleston Place, London SW1W 9NF and Basingstoke.

Associated companies throughout the world.

ISBN 0 7522 1339 3

9 8 7 6 5 4 3 2 1

A CIP catalogue record for this book is available from the British Library.

Printed by The Bath Press

THE SOUTH BANK SHOW

EDITED AND PRESENTED BY

MELVYN BRAGG

2nd December 1997

Oscar Wendlow
  Cleveland Road
Barnes
London SW13 OAA

Dear Oscar Wendlow

I am very sorry that I failed to reply to your first letter. I thought I had done so as
we take great care to reply in this office. First of all the very best of luck to you.
You have chosen a difficult route but I am sure you know what you are doing and it
can be extremely satisfying.

Secondly, I have to decline your kind offer. I simply cannot afford six three hour
sessions as I am working to my absolute limit at the moment.

With best wishes
Yours sincerely

MELVYN BRAGG

 London Weekend Television. The London Television Centre, Upper Ground, London SE1 9LT. Telephone: 0171 620 1620 Fax: 0171 261 3782
Registered in England (No. 2446604) Registered Office: The London Television Centre, Upper Ground, London SE1 9LT

17th October 1997

Peter Stringfellow, Esq.,
Stringfellows,
16-19 Upper St. Martin's Lane,
London, WC2.

Dear Peter Stringfellow,

You are Britain's most successful and well-known nightclub owner (well done!). You are also an innovator who is open to new ideas - you recently brought 'lap-dancing' to the U.K. and it's spreading! A lap-dancing 'joint' opened recently in Hammersmith (not a million miles from where I am sitting this very minute writing you this very letter!). Sadly, I hear it ran into some problems with the local 'constabulary' due to an over-zealous dancer displaying her 'intimate parts' to the 'punters' (shame!).

BUT I DIGRESS! The reason I am writing to you is to offer you a business proposition! I have come up with an idea for a nightclub which I believe is unique and could be HUGE or MEGGA! as they say.

It would be called 'Portraits' and all over the walls there would be pictures of famous people, Humphrey Bogart, Clarke Gable, Marilyn Monroe, Cilla Black etc., AND inside the club there would be a portrait painter positioned at every table sketching the occupants of that table while they chatted and ate their meals. So, at the end of the evening the 'punters' would go home having had a good time AND with their very own portrait under their arm, wrapped in a pretty ribbon!

The club would have a very nice 'creative' atmosphere with the smell of oil crayons wafting through the air. I suggest we even decorate the club like a Parisien artist's 'garret' with beams and bare floorboards and drops of paint splashed everywhere.

Please let me know A.S.A.P. what you think of my idea and <u>please don't discuss it with anyone else!</u>

I was also thinking of trying to get Sir Terence Conran 'on board' to take care of the catering side of things. He has a good track record with food. What do you think?

I look forward to hearing from you very soon and remember, MUM'S THE WORD!

Yours expectantly,

Oscar Wendlow

P.S. I have long been an admirer of yours (I like to see a working-class lad do well) and I happen to know champagne is your favourite 'poison'. I would consider it a privilege if you would have a bottle on me! £10 enclosed. Cheers!!!

29th October, 1997.

Oscar Wendlow,
Portrait Painter to the Stars,
  Cleveland Road,
Barnes,
London,S.W.13 OAA

Dear Oscar,

Thank you for your letter, but I have to say that your suggestion I get involved in your night club is not practical.

I am involved in many projects at the present moment, however, I would like to see you be a success and your idea of trying to get Sir Terance Conran on board is a good one.

Also thank you very much for the ten pounds for Champagne, and I will indeed have a glass of Champagne and toast your future success. However, I would ask you to please accept your £10 back and give to a charity of your choice.

With best wishes,

PETER J. STRINGFELLOW.

Cabaret of Angels

Stringfellows, 16-19 Upper St. Martin's Lane, Covent Garden, London WC2H 9EF Tel 0171 240 5534 Fax 0171 379 3570 Web www.stringfellows.co.uk
Stringfellows is the trading name of Stringfellow Restaurants Ltd. Cabaret of Angels is the trading name of Cabaret of Angels Ltd. Registered Offices 235 Marylebone Road, London NW1 5Q1 Registered No. 2090397 England.

Oscar Wendlow
'Portrait Painter To The Stars'
Cleveland Road, Barnes,
London SW13 OAA

17th October 1997

Sir Terence Conran,

Dear Sir Terence Conran,

I am currently in negotiation with Peter Stringfellow (of Stringfellow's fame) with regard to opening a top West-End nightspot called 'Portraits' and I wondered if you might be interested in a 'piece of the action'.

The basic theme and IMAGE of the club is all sorted, but I thought it might be a good idea to have someone with your experience in catering to provide top-notch meals and snacks! It could also help with raising the financial backing to have a 'Sir' involved in the project.

I can't really say anymore about the club at this stage as it is all very 'HUSH, HUSH', but I would be most grateful if you could let me know 'in principal' if you would be interested in coming 'on board' with me and Peter in this innovative project.

I apologise for the secrecy but the club has a very ORIGINAL theme so we can't go around telling every Tom, Dick and Harry all about it for obvious reasons. I am sure you understand. Once we know you are committed to the project we will be able to tell you more.

I look forward to hearing from you A.S.A.P..

Yours sincerely,

Oscar Wendlow

P.S. I expect it to be VERY profitable and it could be the start of a 'chain'.

TERENCE CONRAN

28 October 1997

Oscar Wendlow
 Cleveland Road
Barnes
London SW13 OAA

Dear Oscar Wendlow

Thank you for your letter and please excuse the delay in replying but I have been abroad.

I'm afraid that current commitments mean that I cannot become involved in your new venture.

Thank you for thinking of me, however.

Yours sincerely

Terence Conran

22nd October 1997

R.Hon. Tony Blair, M.P.,
10 Downing Street,
London,
SW1A.

Dear "Tony",

Please could you do me a favour? Whenever I see you or any other politician speaking to the press outside "Number 10" I am always struck by the incredible shine on the front door as it opens and closes in the background. You can see the television lights reflecting on it like a mirror. It really is the most magnificent paint-job (and I speak as an experienced D.I.Y. man).

Would you be so kind as to let me know what sort of paint was used and/or if the door was given any specialist treatments, i.e. Acrylic Lacquer, French Polish etc.. Also, who was the 'master' responsible for this fine piece of craftsmanship? Obviously I do not expect you to answer this query personally, but I would be most grateful of you could 'pass it on' to the relevant department.

As you can see, I am known as "Portrait Painter to the Stars", however I regret that I am unable to offer to paint your portrait for the simple reason that I am a dyed-in-the-wool Tory and am still feeling 'gutted' about the result of the last Election.

Having said that I must now ask if you would be kind enough to send a signed photograph for my daughter, Anthea. She is a big fan of yours and swears she is going to vote Labour when she is old enough (despite my threats to throw her out of the house - only joking! Ha, ha!). Joyce (my wife) and I think it is just a rebellious phase and she'll grow out of it.

I look forward to hearing from you soon.

Yours sincerely,

Ocar Wendlow

P.S. Just out of interest, are you a D.I.Y. man yourself?

£5 enclosed for party funds from Anthea (she has a Saturday job at the local bakery).

10 DOWNING STREET
LONDON SW1A 2AA

From the Political Office   3 November 1997

Dear Mr Wendlow

Thank you for your letter of 22nd October to the Prime Minister on whose behalf I am replying.

Thank you also for the interest you have shown in Number 10's front door. The finish is obtained by applying up to 15 coats of paint. First the door is primed, then rubbed down using 600 grit paper. Two coats of undercoat are then applied. The first is thinned down, the second is a full coat. The first few coats of gloss are applied after having had thinners and undercoat added. These additions are gradually phased out until the last few coats are neat gloss. I regret I do not have the exact quantities that are used in this process, but hope that the above information is helpful.

I would like to take this opportunity to thank your daughter Anthea for her generous donation of £5 to the Labour Party and as requested I have enclosed a signed photograph of the Prime Minister for her. Contrary to your letter I do not think she is going through a rebellious phase, as you call it, by supporting Labour. Personally I think she is showing signs of very good judgement and maturity!

Thank you for writing.

Yours sincerely,

SARAH GIBSON

Owen Wendlow
Cleveland Road
Barnes
London SW13 0AA

23rd October 1997

William Hague, M.P.,
Conservative Party,
Central Office,
32, Smith Square,
London, SW1 P3HH.

Dear Mr. Hague,

Although I was not 'over the moon' when you were elected party leader I am determined to 'rally' behind you and with this in mind I would like to offer some advice.

When selecting future members of the shadow cabinet I suggest you adopt my very effective "Babysitter Test". It is an extremely efficient method for sorting the 'bad apples' from the 'good eggs'. I invented the technique when our children were small but have continued to utilise it ever since.

When assessing someone's character you simply ask yourself this key question:

WOULD I ALLOW THIS PERSON TO BABYSIT MY CHILDREN?

Here are some examples to illustrate the effectiveness of the method:-

Ken Clark YES	Jonathan Aitken NO
Michael Heseltine YES	Jerry Hayes NO

On the other side of the house:-

Tony Blair YES	Dennis Skinner NO
Mo Mowlem YES	Margaret Beckett NO

It works with overseas politicians too:-

Mikhail Gorbachev YES	Boris Yeltsin NO
Nelson Mandela YES	Saddam Hussein NO

and sports personalities:-

Gary Linneker YES	Paul Gascoine NO
Frank Bruno YES	Mike Tyson NO

I am sure you will agree that these impressive results speak for themselves. I cannot think of a better way of 'weeding out' the bad apples from the 'good eggs', CAN YOU?

I look forward to hearing your comments. Would it be possible to have a signed photo?

Yours sincerely,

Oscar Wendlow

£10 enclosed for party funds.

HOUSE OF COMMONS
LONDON SW1A 0AA

FROM THE OFFICE OF THE LEADER OF THE OPPOSITION

31 October 1997

Dear Mr. Wendlow,

Mr Hague has asked me to thank you for your letter of 23rd October and to reply on his behalf.

It was kind of you to write and Mr Hague is grateful for your support and good wishes. Your generous donation was gratefully received and will go towards our work to make the Conservative Party once again the most effective and professional fighting force in British politics.

Mr Hague will bear your "Babysitter Test" in mind very carefully. I am happy to enclose a signed photograph.

Thank you again for writing.

Yours sincerely,

Kevin Culwick

Oscar Wendlow Esq
'Portrait Painter to the Stars'
  Cleveland Road
Barnes
London
SW13 0AA

Oscar Wendlow
'Portrait Painter To The Stars'
Cleveland Road, Barnes,
London SW13 0AA

Steve Sutherland (Editor)
New Musical Express
25th Floor
Kings Reach Tower
Stamford Street
London SE1 9LS   19th January 1999

Dear Steve Sutherland,

Are you aware of the corrupting influence of your paper, New Musical Express?
Since my son, Raoul started buying it he has undergone a complete character
change and his mother and I are extremely concerned. All his life he has been a
studious and hard-working boy. He has consistently gained excellent marks at
school and in 1997 passed nine GCSE's (two of them A's). He has also been
playing the violin since he was eleven and in 1995 won the Franz Schubert prize
for excellence at the Guildhall Young Musicians Competition. He has also always
been a good-humoured and even-tempered boy.

Then, at the beginning of last year he started buying New Musical Express and his
mother and I started noticing disturbing changes in his behaviour. First it was
purple socks. This was followed by heavy silver rings with ugly motifs such as a
skull and an open mouth with fangs. Then came the new friend, 'Spike' who calls
himself 'a drummer' (I call him a moron). The two of them started answering all
sorts of advertisements in your publication and making rendezvous with God-
knows-who in God-knows-where!

Before we knew it Raoul had bought an electric 'pick up' for his violin and he and
'Spike' had formed a band with the disgusting name of 'Vomit For Breakfast'.
Simultaneously he has gone through a complete character change. He has become
moody, bad tempered, dirty and unhygienic. You practically need a gas mask to go
into his bedroom (which he has painted black!) He also has a new girlfriend called
'Tonka', with a pierced nose, who he refuses to bring in to the house to meet us!

Naturally we are concerned he might be using drugs, although he denies this (he
would, wouldn't he). Fortunately I have a very good friend in the Metropolitan
Police Dogs Division who has kindly agreed to give his bedroom a once-over with
a sniffer dog (it'll probably choke to death on one of his socks!).

You may think it unjust of me to lay blame for all this at your door but we cannot
ignore the fact that the problems began when Raoul started buying your
publication. Are you aware of any other parents who have experienced similar
problems? Do you have an explanation? I sincerely hope you can shed some light
on this very unhappy situation.

Yours sincerely,

Oscar Wendlow

NO REPLY

Oscar Wendlow
'Portrait Painter To The Stars'
Cleveland Road, Barnes,
London SW13 0AA

Tracy Edwards (yachtswoman),   23rd April 1998
c/o Midweek
Room 6906
Broadcasting House
Portland Place
London W1A 1AA

Dear Tracy Edwards,

It was an inspiration to listen to you on Midweek yesterday. What an incredible story! When you were describing the fifty foot wave that smashed your mast and brought down your 'rig' I felt as though I was there with you. I could practically taste the salt on my lips. I don't think the word 'brave' adequately describes the way you and the girls coped - and not a man in sight to take command!

As I listened to your story visualising the mountainous seas and the panic-stricken faces of your crew grappling with the rigging it occurred to me how fantastic it would have been for an artist like myself to have been on board to capture those dramatic moments in 'oils'. Then I heard a little creak in my head. It was the familiar creak of that little 'window of opportunity' opening up. (Remind me to oil it sometime, ha ha !)

You said you are planning another record-breaking voyage around the world and I wondered if next time you might consider taking along an 'artist-in-residence' to record the adventure?

Up to now I have always painted at home in quite constricted circumstances so the thought of getting up on the deck of a boat in the middle of the Atlantic with a six foot by four foot canvas and 'letting rip' with the blues and greys is quite thrilling.
Apart from the on-deck hustle and bustle I would also capture the more intimate moments 'below' with sketches in pencil and pastel ..... the girls doing domestic chores or reading a book, perhaps or putting on their make-up. I am sure you will agree it would make a fantastic exhibition. Please let me know what you think A.S.A.P.

I have always had a love of the sea. Every year we take our holidays in Minehead and nothing gives me greater pleasure than sitting in the T.V. lounge of our hotel staring at it.

I would also be quite happy to 'muck-in' in an emergency. You never know you might find it quite useful having a 'male of the species' aboard.
I greatly look forward to hearing from you and it will certainly be an honour to receive a letter from such a courageous lass.

Yours in anticipation,

Oscar Wendlow

16

Tracy Edwards MBE

Office: 0118 984 4317   Fax: 0118 984 4313
Email: edwards.assoc@easynet.co.uk   website: www.rsachallenge.com

Oscar Wendlow
  Cleveland Road
Barnes
London
SW13 OAA

Dear Oscar

Thank you so much for your kind letter regarding coming on board the catamaran, to sketch the adventures of the girls.

Unfortunately the girls have a 'no men' policy on the boat, but were very grateful of the offer.

Hope you're well and good luck with all your future artwork.

Kind regards,

Claire Higgs
PA to Tracy Edwards

Claire Higgs   7th May 1998

Dear Claire,

Thank you for your letter. I must admit I am disappointed, and don't you think your 'no men' policy is just a little bit sexist?

Having said that, I do appreciate the dangers of mixing the sexes at sea. Tracy is probably afraid of her girls 'falling' for me and competing for my affections which would undermine the 'team spirit'.

Therefore, I would like to offer a solution! Why don't I bring along my other 'alf, Joyce? She's never been sailing before but I'm sure she'd love it. She could also prove quite a useful member of the crew. She's not very fit and she's a few stone overweight so she probably wouldn't be much use on deck but she could certainly 'come into her own' in the 'galley' preparing food and baking cakes (she does a super chilli con carni). What do you think? That way the girls would keep their hands off me and their minds on the sailing

I do hope Tracy will reconsider my offer in the light of this suggestion.

Yours sincerely,

Oscar Wendlow

18

Tracy Edwards

Tel: 0118 9844317   Fax: 0118 9844313
Email: edwards.assoc@easynet.co.uk

Oscar Wendlow
  Cleveland Road
Barnes
London
SW13 OAA

12/05/98

Dear Oscar

Thank you, for letter number two.

Unfortunately by the tone of your letter I now in fact fear for the girls safety, more than anything else, having you on board…only joking.

Seriously Tracy was very grateful for the offer but how could they possibly call themselves an 'all female crew' if they let a male species on the boat.

If anything your letter made us chuckle, and as for your other half, the only thing the girls can have as far as food goes is the freeze dried stuff.

Thanks again for writing, best of luck for the future.

Kind regards,

Claire Higgs
PA to Tracy Edwards

Oscar Wendlow
'Portrait Painter To The Stars'
Cleveland Road, Barnes,
London SW13 0AA

Leslie Waddington, Esq.,
Waddingtons,
11 Cork Street,
London,
W1X 2LT.

21st October 1997

Dear Mr. Waddington,

Having driven down Cork Street and up Clifford Street on numerous occasions in my capacity as a licensed black cab driver I notice that you are the 'proprietor' of more than one gallery (SUCCESSFUL! WELL DONE!) and therefore a good person to approach with regard to putting on an exhibition of my work. Apart from cab driving (it pays the mortgage!) I am also a portrait painter of some two years standing.

At present I am preparing for a major exhibition of my portraits of famous 'personalities' to be titled "BRITISH SUPERSTARS OF THE ARTS AND CULTURE AND POP MUSIC IN BRITAIN AT THE REAR END OF THE NINETIES", and I wondered if you might be interested in putting it on?! I aim to do about 30 paintings of the 'great and the good' and I fully expect them to be my best 'works' to date. I also have 20 not-so-good pictures which I would be happy to 'get rid of' if the price was right. Interested? I will take some snaps of them this weekend and pop them in the post to you or drop them in to your gallery 'in person'. Perhaps we could go-for-a-coffee and talk business!

Please let me know if you are interested in staging my exhibition!

Paintings currently available for sale are listed below.

Yours sincerely,

Ocar Wendlow

1. Joyce (my other 'alf) Watching Coronation Street With Plod (our springer spaniel).
2. Joyce Watching Brookside With Plod.
3. Joyce Watching Coronation Street On Her Own.
4. Joyce, Raoul And Anthea Watching Pretty Woman Video (Triptych)
5. Joyce Watching Crimewatch U.K., Eating Crisps
6. Joyce Watching The Bill In Mohair Jumper
7. Joyce Watching Blind Date, Eating Packet Of Mini Swiss Rolls
8. Raoul Smiling After Getting His G.C.S.E. Results (from photograph)
9. Anthea And Craig Playing Crazy Golf In Torquay (from photograph)
10. Anthea (Laughing) With Plod After Giving Him A Very Short Trim With Clippers (from photograph)
11. Joyce Watching Eastenders, Eating Marshmallows
12. Joyce Reclining On Sofa, Eating Chocolate Mousse With Quizzical Expression
13. Raoul Holding Stool He Made In Woodwork
14. Landscape With Fallen Tree In The Trossachs (Joyce in background preparing picnic)
15. Ted (our neighbour) Holding His Scale Model Of Damon Hill's Williams F1 (from photograph)
16. Joyce Reclining In Garden, Eating Packet of Jaffa Cakes
17. Ted And Margaret Beside Their New Ornamental Fish Pond
18. The Family At Christmas (from photograph)
19. Trevor McDonald (from television)
20. Cilla Black (from television)
21. Joyce Watching Kilroy, Eating Packet of Fig Rolls
22. Joyce Asleep In Front Of Television

All are in oils and unframed

Waddington Galleries

11 CORK STREET LONDON W1X 2LT
TEL: 0171 437 8611 / 439 6262 FAX: 0171 734 4146

HVR/JTH

27th October, 1997

Mr. Oscar Wendlow,
  Cleveland Road,
Barnes,
London, SW13 0AA

Dear Mr. Wendlow,

Thank you for your letter of the 21st October addressed to
Mr. Leslie Waddington, which has been passed on to me.

I am afraid we would not be interested in exhibiting your work but
thank you for your interest in Waddington Galleries.

Yours sincerely,

Hester van Roijen,
Director of Exhibitions

(also 12 & 34 Cork Street) Directors: L.Waddington, A.Bernstein, Sir Thomas Lighton Bt, Lord McAlpine of West Green, H.van Roijen,
S.F.Saunders Registered Number 872520 England. Registered Office: Waddington Galleries Ltd 11 Cork Street London W1X 2LT

Oscar Wendlow
'Portrait Painter To The Stars'
Cleveland Road, Barnes,
London SW13 0AA

3rd November 1997

Camelot Foundation,
1 Derry Street,
London,
W8 5HY.

Dear Camelot,

I would like to apply for £100,000 lottery funding for my proposed exhibition "BRITISH SUPERSTARS OF THE ARTS AND CULTURE AND MUSIC IN BRITAIN AT THE REAR END OF THE NINETIES" which will be held at a 'top' West End gallery.

I am not a full-time artist YET! I drive a cab "for my sins" but I would need to take a year off to concentrate on the exhibition. I reckon I would also need a capable assistant and money for materials. Here is a detailed breakdown of costs:-

£50,000.00 to compensate for loss of earnings
£30,000.00 my assistant, Joyce
£10,000.00 materials
£10,000.00 'sundries'/unexpected 'extras'
£100,000.00

I hope you will consider this application favourably. It will be a major contribution to the cultural life of GREAT BRITAIN at the end of the millennium. And this is REAL ART! NOT that dead cows in formaldehyde and empty houses filled with concrete CRAP!

Yours sincerely,

Ocar Wardlow

P.S. Please do not send cheque in post. Contact me at the above for bank details.

Oscar Wendlow
'Portrait Painter To The Stars'
Cleveland Road, Barnes,
London SW13 0AA

Camelot Foundation,
1 Derry Street,
London,
W8 5HY.

23rd November 1997

Dear Camelot,

On 3rd November I sent you an application for £100,000 funding for my proposed exhibition 'BRITISH SUPERSTARS OF THE ARTS AND CULTURE AND MUSIC IN BRITAIN AT THE REAR END OF THE NINETIES'. Since then I have heard nothing from you.

As you will appreciate it is very difficult for me to plan ahead when I don't know if I am getting the money or not. Joyce, my wife (and assistant) usually books our summer holiday in Minehead at this time of year. However, if we knew we had a hundred 'grand' coming our way we would probably go to Florida or on a cruise. I also have to make arrangements with people to 'sit' for me to paint their portraits.

Could you please let me know how my application is progressing!!!

Yours sincerely,

Oscar Wendlow

THE CAMELOT FOUNDATION
ONE DERRY STREET LONDON W8 5HY
TEL: 0171 937 5594 FAX: 0171 937 0574
MINICOM: 0171 937 5471

25 November 1997

Mr Oscar Wendlow
'Portrait Painter To The Stars'
  Cleveland Road
Barnes
London SW13 0AA

Dear Mr Wendlow

Thank you for your letter of 3 November 1997 and for your follow up letter, received here on 24 November 1997. I apologise for the delay in replying to you.

The Camelot Foundation's Community Support Programme is only able to fund organisations whose work is charitable and it is not able to fund requests from individuals. Its funding priorities are disadvantage and disability. I am afraid that we will, therefore, not be able to help you.

My advice would be to contact The Arts Council on 0171 312 0123 or to go to the reference section of your local library to see if they have a directory of arts funding organisations, such as The Arts Funding Guide, produced by The Directory of Social Change. If your library does not have a copy it costs about £16 and DoSC's telephone number is 0171 209 5151.

I am sorry to send you such a disappointing letter and I wish you success in your fund-raising and in your work.

Yours sincerely

Martin Jones
Community Support Manager.

Oscar Wendlow
'Portrait Painter To The Stars'
Cleveland Road, Barnes,
London SW13 0AA

20th October 1997

Ms. Sue Lawley,
'Desert Island Discs',
Room 6089,
Broadcasting House,
Portland Place,
London,
W1A 1AA.

Dear Sue Lawley,

Thank you for the pleasure you give each week with 'Desert Island Discs'. I am sure Roy Plomley (its' creator) would be 'chuffed to bits' with your performance were he not dead.

I am actually writing to ask if you would consider having a 'mere mortal' like myself on the show?

Believe it or not 'ordinary-men-in-the-street' often have far more interesting lives than the so-called 'rich and famous'! Take ME for example. I have been a licensed black cab-driver for some 23 years now, and I could tell you stories that would make your hairs curl. Plus a 'VERITABLE PLETHORA' of anecdotes about famous people I have picked up including Sir Lawrence Olivier (before he died), Patrick Moore (the astrologer) and Paul Daniels (a real gentleman!).

I once saved a man from drowning after he drove his Range Rover into the Thames at Putney! I was outside the Old Bailey when the Guildford Four were released! (crowds). I got caught up in the Poll Tax riots and had my rear windscreen smashed! Etc., etc., etc..

I am also a man of many parts; I write poetry, and have had two published in 'Cab Driver' (proud!). I have written two plays:

DEATH OF A MINICAB DRIVER
and
HE WAS A 'CHARACTER',

a fictionalised story about a cab driver named 'Big Jim Mulligan'. I have written songs and 'last' but by no means 'least' I paint in oils. I am currently putting together an exhibition of portraits of British Superstars of the 'arts' and 'media'. If you invite me on 'Desert Island Discs' I would certainly like to include you in my exhibition! It will be held at a top West-End gallery with a private view with free wine and crisps etc..

Incidentally, my 'discs' for the show would be a cross section of Carpenters, Shadows, Beatles, Rod Stewart, Roy Orbison and Elvis (THE KING, not that Costello prat!).

I look forward to hearing from you and hope that we can 'do business'.

Yours sincerely,

Oscar Wendlow

P.S. People WANT to hear about ordinary folk. NOT STARS ALL THE TIME!

BRITISH BROADCASTING CORPORATION
BROADCASTING HOUSE
PORTLAND PLACE
LONDON W1A 1AA
TELEPHONE: 0171-580 4468

10th November 1997

Dear Oscar Wendlow

Thank you for your letter of 7th November and for your suggestion of yourself as a castaway on Desert Island Discs. I am sorry a reply wasn't forthcoming after your initial letter in October, but as I am sure you must know, we get a great many offers of guests wanting to appear on the programme. Often these are from agents who are used to no reply indicating that their client is not for us. Of course as a private individual you are not in this business and I must apologise for not getting back to you quicker.

I am sorry to disappoint you but the brief of the programme is to interview well-known people who have made a singular contribution in their chosen field. While we recognise that many 'ordinary' people have led very interesting lives, Desert Island Discs is not really the forum for them.

Thank you once again for your letters, and I do hope you continue to enjoy Desert Island Discs.

Yours sincerely,

Julie Batty
Researcher, Desert Island Discs

Oscar Wendlow
'Portrait Painter To The Stars'
Cleveland Road, Barnes,
London SW13 0AA

4th November 1997

Marks & Spencer Plc.,
Michael House,
47, Baker Street,
London,
W1A 1DN.

To Whom It May Concern,

In May of this year my wife purchased (on my behalf) two pairs of dark blue cotton/polyester mix socks from your Kingston branch. About six weeks later she began to notice that whenever she was pairing them off after washing, there seemed to be one sock left over. She put it to one side hoping she would soon find it's 'mate' but to no avail. Eventually we gave the house a thorough top to bottom search but still there was no sign of the missing sock.

It was then that Joyce (my other 'alf) reminded me that exactly the same problem had befallen us the year before with another sock, and guess where it was purchased...! THAT'S RIGHT! MARKS AND SPENCER!

I am sure you will agree that two of your socks going missing in the space of twelve months is wholly unacceptable and not what one expects of a high quality Marks and Spencer product.

I look forward to receiving an apology and hopefully some form of recompense.

This never happened when I bought my socks at C & A.

Yours sincerely,

P.S. I initially planned to send the leftover sock to the victims of landmines but have decided to send it to you instead as proof!

MARKS & SPENCER

Mr O Wendlow
Cleveland Road
Barnes
London
SW13 0AA

05 November 1997

Our Ref: YP/1655896/001/TG

Dear Mr Wendlow

Thank you for returning the socks. I am sorry that you were disappointed with these items.

I have examined the socks but have been unable to establish any form of manufacturing fault. I am afraid Marks & Spencer cannot be held responsible for the loss of the socks, even though this problem has not ocurred with socks of other manufacturors. However, I can appreciate how frustrating it is when a product does not meet your expectations and, as such, I am enclosing a refund of £10.00.

Thank you for taking the time and trouble to contact us, and I do hope that any future purchases you make from our stores prove entirely satisfactory.

Yours sincerely

YOGINI PATEL
Customer Adviser
0171 268 1234

St Mi...
THE BRAND NAME OF

PRODUCED ON RECYCLED PAPER

REGISTERED OFFICE: MICHAEL HOUSE ·
REGISTERED NO. 214436 (EN...

29

Oscar Wendlow
'Portrait Painter To The Stars'
Cleveland Road, Barnes,
London SW13 0AA

Jonathan Cainer (Astrologer), Esq.,
The Daily Mail,
Northcliffe House,
2 Derry Street,
London,
W8 5TS.   16th October 1997

Dear Jonathan Cainer,

I don't believe in astrology but I must admit I do sometimes read your predictions in the Mail every day and occasionally I call your telephone horoscope line every weekend. I regard it as a harmless bit of fun, a 'giggle'.

However, the other week your predictions were so inaccurate I felt compelled to complain.

You said if I was prepared to "have faith" and "believe good things could happen" they would! You said it would be a week of "exciting opportunities" and that I would meet people who would "help further my goals". In summing up you said it was going to be a "wondrous week" and that everything I did would be "touched by magic".

As you can imagine I felt 'chuffed to bits' after hearing that lot. Then, guess what happened! Having carefully placed my paint palette, (I am an artist) on the settee to call you, my wife, Joyce, sat on it, spreading paint all over the cream cushions. While I tried to clean it off with white spirit she forgot she had paint all over her 'posterior' and sat down AGAIN on the cream-coloured ARMCHAIR! BRILLIANT! Two cushions ruined with brown paint (I was painting Trevor McDonald, the newscaster at the time). THEN, GUESS WHAT!

My son Raoul rings up in tears to tell me he has had an accident in MY CAR in the CAR PARK of Sainsbury's Homebase in Richmond (he was getting me some rawlplugs) and that his girlfriend, "Gabby", has been taken to hospital with 'WHIPLASH'. On the Monday our dog, Plod, got run-over by a hit-and-run roller-blader - one dislocated shoulder. One £160 vet bill! On Tuesday Joyce found some pills in Raoul's bedroom which turned out to be "ECSTASY". On Thursday my daughter Anthea was 'DUMPED' by her fiance, "Craig", and on Friday a dozy cow in a 4x4 drove into the back of my cab (I am a cab-driver as well as an artist) making it un-roadworthy. WELL, JONATHAN? WHAT HAVE YOU GOT TO SAY FOR YOURSELF? I think the very least you can do is apologise.

Yours sincerely,

Ocar Wendlow

JONATHAN CAINER
Horoscope Service

Oscar Wendlow
  Cleveland Rd
Barnes
London
SW13 0AA

14 November, 1997

Dear Oscar

Thank you for your letter. Now that Jonathan is writing for the Daily Mail as well as Prima and Woman magazines, he has been receiving so many letters that in order to be able to answer them all personally, he has devised a system whereby he read his letters and then lets me know what he would like to say in reply.

You have asked Jonathan why the happy events mentioned in his forecast for you the other week failed to materialise. In response Jonathan says that there are certain times in everyone's lives when extenuating circumstances in their personal charts override the planetary influences of their Sun sign alone.

Jonathan goes on to explain that it was the uncanny accuracy of Patric Walker's column which provided him with the inspiration of becoming an astrologer himself However, whilst there were many times when it would almost seem as though Patric was looking over his shoulder, there would be others when he didn't seem to know him from Adam. Jonathan brought up this point with Patric, they discussed it in depth and came to the conclusion that there will always be certain times in one's life when powerful planetary aspects taking place in one's personal horoscope take precedence over the day to day functioning of the Sun sign. Once the dust has settled and some sort of normality is resumed, even if it is a different normality to how things were previously, then the Sun sign gradually kicks in again.

Jonathan hopes this helps to shed some light on your query and that you'll continue to keep in touch with his forecasts - either by calling the zodiac line or through his regular columns. Please feel free to write in again with any further comments or questions.

Best wishes

pp Jonathan Cainer

Oscar Wendlow
'Portrait Painter To The Stars'
Cleveland Road, Barnes,
London SW13 0AA

31st October 1997

Michael Heseltine, M.P.,
House of Commons,
Westminster,
London,
SW1A 2PW.

Dear Michael Heseltine,

I must say how much I miss your 'presence' on the contemporary political stage. I have long cherished the idea that you might one day become party leader and that hope remains un-dimmed. I don't wish to be unkind to William Hague but LET'S BE HONEST, he doesn't exactly inspire confidence, does he?

What we need in the driving seat is a 'HEAVYWEIGHT', A STATESMANLIKE figure with 'EXPERIENCE' and 'CHARISMA'! Someone called MICHAEL HESELTINE!!!

It is with this in mind that I am writing to you today.

Your problem is that people see you as cold, aloof and uncaring. I would like to help you change that perception by painting an 'informal' picture of you depicting you as a 'man of the people'. You could then offer the picture to the press for publication.

What I have in mind is a relaxed outdoor pose with a Michael Heseltine-relaxing-at-the-weekend feel to it. I imagine you NOT on your magnificent Essex estate but in a council housing estate in Brixton or the East End perhaps. You would be smiling and wearing NOT your usual elegant politician's attire but the kind of 'clobber' the ordinary man in the street can relate to, a pair of training shoes perhaps and a pair of tracksuit bottoms or jeans. On top you could be wearing a T-shirt with a contemporary slogan, 'Oasis' perhaps or 'Save The Whale'. It is important to reflect your hobbies so perhaps you could have a shotgun over your arm and a 'brace' of dead pheasants at your feet. I thought we could also have a couple of red 'dispatch' boxes at your feet to denote POWER and a small crowd of 'mixed-race' children behind you, smiling to suggest harmony and racial integration.

This could be the beginning of a new lease of life for your political career! Let me know what you think and if you are interested we can arrange some 'sittings'. I WANT TO SEE MICHAEL HESELTINE AT NUMBER 10! LET'S GET TO WORK!

Yours sincerely,

Ocar Wendlow

£20 enclosed for party funds

HOUSE OF COMMONS

LONDON SW1A 0AA

21st November 1997

Oscar Wendlow Esq
  Cleveland Road
Barnes
London SWl3 OAA

Dear Mr Wendlow,

Thank you very much for your letter of 31st October.

I appreciate your kind remarks, but I have no plans at the moment to commission a portrait.

It was good of you to send £20 for party funds and I have sent this on to the treasurer of the Conservative Party.

Your sincerely,

The Rt Hon Michael Heseltine CH MP

Oscar Wendlow
'Portrait Painter To The Stars'
Cleveland Road, Barnes,
London SW13 0AA

19th October 1997

Peter Mandelson, M.P.,
House of Commons,
Westminster,
London,
SW1A 2PW.

Dear Peter Mandelson,

I am writing to protest about the outrageous cost of the proposed 'Millennium Dome'. What a scandalous waste of money! And who wants it? NOBODY! It's going to be a 'white elephant'! Think of the schools you could build with £758 million! Or hospitals! Or Kidney Units! Or Variety Club mini-buses! Or homes for the elderly and homeless! I thought Labour was supposed to be the party of caring, compassion, NOT wasteful expense!

Nevertheless, if you do decide to ignore public opinion and GO AHEAD with the Dome I would be interested in getting involved. As you can see from my letterhead I am a bit of a dab-hand with the old 'oils' and I have an idea that may appeal to you and your committee. How about turning the inside of the Dome into a huge Cistine Chapel-type mural? What I have in mind is the faces of all the significant 'characters' in culture, politics and sport over the last hundred years. From Lloyd George to Elton John.. From Winston Churchill to Frank Bruno. From Sir Malcolm Sargent to Cilla Black. The faces would blend together into a huge Spanish omelette of fame, talent, charisma and history!

If you are interested I could do some 'roughs' and drop them off to you 'personally'.

I reckon we would need at least 100 artists to execute the job and it would take about 3 months. My cousin has a good friend, Barry, who runs a paint shop in Billericay in Essex who could get you a 'good deal' on a BIG order of paint!

I reckon you would need to pay the artists about £60 per day and I would want £200 per day to compensate for loss of earnings. Don't worry about catering, Joyce (my wife) makes me sandwiches for work every day as it is (cheese and onion, my all-time favourite).

My only concern is if we can find 100 'capable' painters. It seems all they learn at art school these days is 'dead cows in formaldahyde'. We can cross that bridge when we get to it, Peter! I hope you like my idea and look forward to hearing from you A.S.A.P..

Yours sincerely,

Ocar Wendlow

P.S. You would be included in the painting! (In case you were wondering)
P.P.S. HURRY UP! TIME IS RUNNING OUT!

M The New Millennium Experience Company Ltd

110 Buckingham Palace Road Tel: 0171 808 8200
London SW1W 9SB Fax: 0171 808 8240

24 November 1997

Oscar Wendlow Esq.
'Portrait Artist to the Stars'
  Cleveland Road
Barnes
London SW13 0AA

Our ref: 101997

Dear Mr Wendlow,

RE: Mural on the inside of the Dome.

Thank you for your letter of 18 November, which has been passed to me for reply.

We have now carefully reviewed all proposals to date. As you can appreciate, we have received an enormous number of proposals, some of which include similar ideas to your own. However, I am afraid that your concept is one we are unable to progress with.

I would like to take this opportunity to wish you every success and thank you very much for your interest in the Millennium Experience. We hope you will join us in Greenwich in the year 2000, for what we plan to be a great event.

Yours sincerely,

Lucy Liemann.

Lucy Liemann
Implementation Department.

Oscar Wendlow
'Portrait Painter To The Stars'
Cleveland Road, Barnes,
London SW13 0AA

15th October 1997

The Met Office (Complaints),
London Road,
Bracknell,
Berkshire, RG2 2SZ.

To Whom it May Concern,

On Tuesday 23rd September we had a fine sunny day here in London. I made a point of watching the weather forecast on television that night as I wanted to make plans for the rest of the week. The BBC weatherman who follows the nine o'clock news (I think it was Michael Cockroft) stated CATEGORICALLY that the fine weather would 'continue to the end of the week.' 'Marvellous', we thought, and on that basis I called my brother Maurice and told him he could have my cab until the end of the week (we are both cab drivers and his is temporarily off the road). As fine weather had been assured I decided to go for a few days landscape painting in the 'Trossachs' with my wife, Joyce (she doesn't paint but she's happy to sit and watch me so long as she's got something to suck - peppermints are her weakness). Maurice said 'OKAY MATE, TA VERY MUCH!' and Joyce and I started packing our bags.

Well, GUESS WHAT! We spent three days under heavy grey clouds and drizzle. Joyce caught a nasty cold and is coughing up phlegm AS I WRITE! I had three pastel sketches ruined. One of them I was particularly pleased with, of a herd of young bulls under an oak tree, titled 'Bullocks in the Trossachs', ended up looking like a herd of sheep on stilts.

THANK YOU VERY MUCH FOR RUINING OUR BREAK WITH YOUR COMPLETELY INACCURATE WEATHER FORECAST!

I calculate that with loss of earnings, B & B, meals, snacks, peppermints and petrol that the whole trip must have cost about £950. WHAT A WASTE OF MONEY!

I am hoping to spend the weekend of the 25th and 26th of October on the North Downs painting 'Rural Scene with Plod' (our springer spaniel - he looks like a special branch detective).

Can you PLEASE make sure we have some fine weather on those days?!

I would also appreciate some sort of apology for our ruined holiday, perhaps from Michael Cockroft himself!

Yours sincerely,

Oscar Wendlow

P.S. What's the point of having weather forecasts if they are wrong? If a customer asks me to take him to Waterloo Station I don't take him to the Albert Hall, do I?!!

The Met.Office

The Meteorological Office
Enquiries Office, Room 709
London Road, Bracknell
Berkshire RG12 2SZ
United Kingdom

Tel: 01344 854455
International:
        +44 1344 854455
Fax: 01344 854942
Telex: 849801

Oscar Wendlow
  Cleveland Road
Barnes
London
SW13 0AA

Our Ref: M/M/8/4/4

21st October 1997

Dear Mr Wendlow,

Thank you for your letter, dated the 15th October, which only arrived here today.   I am sorry that you seem to have had such a wretched holiday in the Trossachs in late September, and that this was not apparently forecast.

Unfortunately, I was out of the country myself at the time, enjoying some glorious weather in Germany, and cannot relate to the occasion and circumstances that you have referred to. Had you written nearer the time, a colleague who might have remembered the events of the time, might have been able to give you a more comprehensive response. As it is, all I have to go on is a transcript of the BBC Radio 4 1755 forecast. These Radio 4 forecasts are prepared at the BBC Weather Centre by the same team as the TV forecasts, so this script - attached - might well have been written by Peter Cockcroft, although I cannot tell.   I agree that the implication of that was that fine weather was expected to cover all but the far north for the rest of the week.   However, it did mention that cloud cover would be a problem.   I have looked at the charts for the following few days and, in the event, that part of Scotland was afflicted with persistent cloud. Although none of our observing stations reported any drizzle, I do not dispute that there would have been some 'up-slope' drizzly rain on hills facing the wind. I have to say that had you travelled just a few miles, then things would have been much better.

So what further can I say ?   Meteorology remains an imprecise 'science' and we can only do our best using whatever information we have to hand at the time. The atmosphere is extremely complex and behaves in a fairly random manner which even the World's most powerful super-computers cannot fully handle. And one should also realise that the TV and radio people on the BBC get their core guidance from this HQ at Bracknell, so when things go wrong it is us that should be blamed, not them.

You ask what is the point of having weather forecasts if they are wrong. Well, none whatsoever if this was always the case.   The fact is that most of our shorter term forecasts, for the next couple of days or so, do give good advice.   As I stated above, we all have to accept that sometimes sudden and unexpected developments can cause things to go awry, and once they have started to go wrong, they will not right themselves. Therefore, the longer range 5-day forecasts are not so successful as the 2-day ones, but they can be taken as trend forecasts, so long as exact detail is not required.

Finally, you have used the analogy of your profession always taking passengers where they want to go. This is not a fair comparison, as locations are fixed and do not change, unlike the features and physics of the atmosphere. Even taxi drivers cannot always say just how long it will take to reach their destination as unknowns such as accidents, roadworks and other holdups, not to mention breakdowns, can all affect the journey time. And this too can cost the punter dearly as the meter ticks on relentlessly. But it's no good at all complaining ! It's just a fact of life.

As for this coming weekend, it does seem that high pressure will dominate the country so the North Downs should be dry. But at this time of year don't expect miracles. It is late October and this means that quiet clear nights can lead to frost and fog forming, some of which can linger well into the mornings. But I don't expect it will worry Plod.

Yours sincerely

D. C. Hardy

Derek Hardy   (Enquiries Officer)

Sep 97

FPUK43 EGRR 241417
BROADCAST AT 231755

GOOD EVENING. AT THE MOMENT WE HAVE AN AREA OF HIGH PRESSURE OVER THE NORTH SEA. THE CHARTS RIGHT UP TO THE END OF THE WEEK, FOR THE WEEK-END, SHOW THAT HIGH PRESSURE STILL THERE. I THINK WE SHALL SEE A WEAK FRONT APPROACH SCOTLAND DURING THURSDAY AND FRIDAY. THE MAIN CHALLENGE OVER THE NEXT FEW DAYS IS FORECASTING THE AMOUNTS OF CLOUD. THAT REALLY IS A VERY STIFF CHALLENGE INDEED.

ENGLAND AND WALES - MANY PLACES OVERNIGHT WILL STAY QUITE CLEAR BUT ... SOUTHWEST OF ... ANY PATCHY CLOUD ... DAY. SOME SUNSHINE, A BRIGHTER DAY ... COASTAL TEMP 15-17, BUT 18-20

THE NEXT COUPLE OF DAYS - STAYING DRY OVER ENGLAND AND WALES BUT IN THE NORTH OF SCOTLAND SOME PATCHY RAIN PARTICULARLY ON THURSDAY.

The Met.Office

London Road Bracknell Berkshire RG12 2SZ
Switchboard: +44 (0)1344 420242

Tel: +44(0)1344 854629
Fax: +44(0)1344 854942
e-mail: acyeatman@meto.gov.uk

Ref : 8/4/4

3 November 1997

Mr Oscar Wendlow
  Cleveland Road
Barnes
London
SW13 0AA

Dear Mr Wendlow

You recently had occasion to write a letter of complaint to The Met. Office . At The Met. Office we take these complaints, and the way we handle them very seriously. To monitor our response to complaints, I am asking for a few minutes of your time to answer the following questions, and then return the whole letter to me in the enclosed reply paid envelope.

Are you happy with the time taken by The Met. Office to reply to your complaint?

Yes, the reply came by 'return of post.'

Are you happy with the way that our Enquiries Officer has dealt with your complaint?

Not really. I would have been much happier if I had received a reply from the 'organ grinder' (Michael Cockroft) instead of his 'monkey'. Also I sensed he was making 'light' of my complaint.

**Are there any other comments that you would like to make about the way
The Met. Office has handled your complaint?**

Yes, you ignored my request for sunny weather over the north downs on the 25th and 26th October. It was a thoroughly miserable weekend, made worse by my dog, Plod rolling in something 'unpleasant', but that's not your fault. More sunshine please !!!

Thank you in anticipation of your answers to these questions.

Yours sincerely

Yeatman

Andy Yeatman, Senior Press Officer

Oscar Wendlow
'Portrait Painter To The Stars'
Cleveland Road, Barnes,
London SW13 0AA

16th October 1997

Trevor McDonald (newsreader), Esq.,
ITN News,
200, Grays' Inn Road,
London,
WC1X 8XZ.

Dear Trevor McDonald,

My wife and I are big fans of yours but I must admit you are not in my 'best books' TODAY!

I am a big fan of Chelsea Football Club and last night I was looking forward to watching highlights of their game with Blackburn on Carlton Sport, after the news.

BUT, at the end of the news you did the football scores and said "If you don't want to know the result look away now!"

That is exactly what I did but I happened to look straight into our glass-fronted 'cocktail cabinet' and in the glass I saw this reflection:

CHELSEA 4
BLACKBURN 1

(shown mirror-reversed)

THANK YOU FOR COMPLETELY RUINING MY EVENING'S ENTERTAINMENT, TREVOR! Might I suggest that in future you say, "If you don't want to know the result CLOSE YOUR EYES"!!!

An apology would be appreciated.

Yours sincerely,

Ocar Wendlow

200 Gray's Inn Road
London WC1X 8XZ
Telephone 0171 833 3000

Oscar Wendlow
  Cleveland Road
Barnes
London
SW13 0AA

25 November 1997

Dear Mr Wendlow

I must confess that when I got this letter the first time around I did not take it seriously. It seems to me that what is called for is something to cover up your glass-fronted cocktail cabinet.

However, your second letter leads me to think that this has affected you very deeply. We are very sorry.

The subject of football results has engaged our interest for some 20 years now, and we still don't always get it right. We shall give earnest consideration to your suggestion.

Yours sincerely

Trevor McDonald

Registered Office 200 Gray's Inn Road London WC1X 8XZ Registered Number 548648 England
Independent Television News Limited

Oscar Wendlow
'Portrait Painter To The Stars'
Cleveland Road, Barnes,
London SW13 0AA

1st November 1997

Hilary Davis,
Road Safety Division,
Department of Transport,
Zone 2/4,
Great Minster House,
76 Marshall Street,
London,
SW1P 4DR.

Dear Hilary Davis,

Having been a licensed black-cab driver for some 22 years I would like to make a suggestion in the interest of road safety.

I have noticed for a long time that the green light on traffic lights indicating "GO" is brighter than the amber and red lights. Surely this is WRONG! In the interests of road safety shouldn't the light which indicates "STOP" be the brighter of the three? OF COURSE IT SHOULD!!

I therefore suggest you consider reversing the order of all traffic lights with the red light at the bottom to indicate "GO", the amber light remaining in the middle denoting "CAUTION - LIGHTS CHANGING" and the green light at the top indicating "STOP. Perhaps you could run some trials on a few randomly selected sets of traffic lights.

I realise it might cause some confusion at first but in the long-term I believe it could result in a reduction in people 'shooting' the lights and causing serious accidents.

Please let me know your thoughts on my suggestion (which is based on many years' motoring experience).

Yours sincerely,

Ocar Wendlow

Department of the Environment, Transport and the Regions

DRIVER INFORMATION AND TRAFFIC
MANAGEMENT DIVISION
3/25 GREAT MINSTER HOUSE
76 MARSHAM STREET
LONDON SW1P 4DR

Mr O Wendlow
  Cleveland Road
Barnes
LONDON
SW13 0AA

OUR REF: RED 12/4/01
YOUR REF:

13 NOVEMBER 1997

Dear Mr Wendlow

POSITION OF LANTERNS IN TRAFFIC LIGHT SIGNAL HEADS

Thank you for your letter, dated 1 November, regarding the above.

I think the first point to make, which applies to signs in general, is that because of our reading practice people scan from top to bottom and it is normal to put the most important message at the top.

Specifically for traffic lights there are practical advantages gained by having the red lantern in the present position. It is the most conspicuous in circumstances where the visibility is impaired by other vehicles or the physical road layout and the least vulnerable to grime and attack from vandals.

The present layout was introduced in the 1920/30's and I believe that in the majority of countries using traffic lights have the red at the top. Over the years the colour of the containers has changed as has the intensity of the lanterns. In the 1970's the source of light was changed from tungsten to tungsten halogen. All three lanterns are illuminated using the same wattage lamp.

Drivers perception of colour and brightness varies greatly. One of the original arguments for consistency of design was the surprising number of drivers who are "colour blind", or more accurately colour defective. The position of the lantern, relative to the others, is therefore very important and would rule out any piecemeal change. Indeed, because it is now common for many drivers to travel extensively, it would not be safe for one country to take unilateral action.

Reversing the position of the red and green lanterns may have an advantage but I believe the disadvantages weigh heavily in favour of keeping the present system.

Yours sincerely,

M R MIDDLETON

Oscar Wendlow
'Portrait Painter To The Stars'
Cleveland Road, Barnes,
London SW13 0AA

3rd November 1997

The Editor,
The Daily Telegraph,
1 Canada Square,
Canary Wharf,
London,
E14 5DT.

Dear Sir,

Is this sort of advertising really necessary in a family newspaper?

Yours sincerely,

Oscar Wendlow

Oscar Wendlow
'Portrait Painter To The Stars'
Cleveland Road, Barnes,
London SW13 0AA

H.R.H. Princess Margaret,
N.S.P.C.C.,
42, Curtain Road,
London,
EC2A 3NH.

2nd November 1997

Your Royal Highness,

If the name looks familiar it is because I am a regular contributor to your very worthy charity. Sadly, on this occasion I am writing to you as a 'concerned neighbour'.

About 18 months ago a new family bought the house next-door. They seemed nice enough although we are fed up with the noise and mess of their builders. Also the conservatory they have built spoils the view from our kitchen window and their loft conversion blocks the sunlight from our garden. Also, they take up TWO parking spaces with their Jeep and their BMW (Pat, the old dear who used to live there never even HAD a car!). BUT I DIGRESS!

I am actually writing to you because I am concerned about the welfare of their children.

<u>Can the name a parent gives a child constitute an act of cruelty</u>? If so there is wanton cruelty going on next-door! Their children are called... wait for it... 'Caspar', 'Horatio' and 'Pomegranite'. <u>TRUE</u>!

My wife bumped into the parents, 'Hugo' and 'Lettice', this morning who revealed they are expecting ANOTHER baby (whatever happened to good old-fashioned contraception?) which they intend to call either 'Columbus' or 'Muff' depending on its' sex.

I do not like to think of myself as an interfering neighbour but I am concerned for these poor 'nippers'. Could they be renamed by law? Should the parents be prosecuted?

Yours sincerely,

Ocar Wendlow

P.S. I BLAME PAULA YATES AND "SIR BOB"! THEY STARTED IT!

£40 contribution enclosed

0171-930 3141

KENSINGTON PALACE
W8 4PU

From: Lord Napier and Ettrick, KCVO.

7th November, 1997

Dear Mr. Wendlow.

    Princess Margaret has asked me write to thank you for your letter of 2nd November, and for the very kind donation of £40.00 which you enclosed for the NSPCC.

    This has been forwarded to the Society's Headquarters, and the matter about which you write has been brought to their attention.

Private Secretary to
The Princess Margaret,
Countess of Snowdon.

Oscar Wendlow, Esq.

NSPCC

Our Ref : MT/mbs

The National Society
for the Prevention of
Cruelty to Children

National Centre,
42 Curtain Road,
London EC2A 3NH
Telephone: 0171-825 2500
Fax: 0171-825 2525
Direct line: 0171-825

4th December 1997

Mr O Wendlow
   Cleveland Road
Barnes
SW13 0AA

Dear Mr Wendlow

Your letter of 2nd November addressed to our President has been passed through to me as you were advised in the letter of 7th November from the Private Secretary.

I would like to add my thanks for the generous donation which you have made to our work.

As regards the names of children, I can only advise that there is no case in law for authorities taking action to stop the unfortunate decisions of parents. We appear to have moved from whole football teams to rather outlandish Christian names. Young people can, and do, decide which name they wish to use and often a shortened version or a nickname suffices. The name can be changed legally in later years.

With best wishes

Yours sincerely

Mike Taylor
Director of Operations

The NSPCC works to prevent cruelty to children and is dependent upon voluntary donations for its existence.

Patrons: Her Majesty The Queen, Her Majesty Queen Elizabeth The Queen Mother.
President: Her Royal Highness The Princess Margaret Countess of Snowdon.
Chairman: John Norton.
Director & Chief Executive: Jim Harding.
Founded 1884. Incorporated by Royal Charter. Registered Charity No. 216401.

Code 0358

RECYCLED PAPER

Robin Cook MP   3rd May 1998
Foreign Secretary
House of Commons
Westminster
London SW1A 2PW

Dear Mr Cook,

My wife has been nagging me to grow a beard for some time as she thinks it will make me look more 'distinguished'. I have finally agreed (they always get their way in the end, don't they) and from Sunday I am going to stop shaving. We both think that as beards go yours is a fine specimen and the sort of shape and length I should 'go for'. Would you be so kind as to answer the following questions so that I can hopefully achieve the 'Robin Cook look';

A. Do you trim it with scissors or an electric beard trimmer? If so, what make?
B. How often do you trim it?
C. Do you wash it every time you wash your hair? Every day?
D. Do you use shampoo or face soap?
E. Does it make you hotter in the summer?

I must confess I am not a labour supporter but I hope that wont prejudice your response. My daughter, Anthea is a huge fan of yours and has asked me to enclose £10 of her own money for party funds. She also asks if it would be possible for you to send her a signed photo?

Congratulations on your recent 'nuptials'. I wish you and your secretary every happiness, and don't worry too much about your ex-wife, time is a great healer.

Best wishes from a true-blue tory,

Oscar Wendlow

**Foreign &
Commonwealth
Office**

London SW1A 2AH

07 May 1998

Dear Mr Wendlow,

Thank you for your letter addressed to the Foreign Secretary dated 3 May.

We are not able to accept your kind contribution of £10 (enclosed) to the Labour Party but suggest that you send your donation direct to the Parliamentary Labour Party Resource Centre, House of Commons, London SW1A 2AA.

I will be very happy to send a signed photograph of Mr Cook in due course.

I have passed on your good wishes to the Foreign Secretary and Mrs Cook.

Yours Sincerely,

Lynne Rossiter

Lynne Rossiter
Assistant Private Secretary

Oscar Wendlow Esq

Oscar Wendlow
'Portrait Painter To The Stars'
Cleveland Road, Barnes,
London SW13 0AA

The Garrick Club,
15, Garrick St.
London WC2E 9AY   1st October 1998

To whom it may concern,

I am interested in becoming a member of your club which I believe is
popular with people of an artistic 'bent'. As you can see from my heading
I am a painter myself (between driving a cab and bringing up two bone-
idle teenagers, ha, ha!) and am currently working on a 'high-profile'
exhibition as part of the millennium celebrations.

Would you be so kind as to send me an 'application form' and let me
know the membership fees.

Yours sincerely,

Oscar Wendlow

Secretary's Office.

Telephone:
0171-836 1737

Garrick Club,
Garrick Street,
WC2E 9AY.

O Wendlow Esq
 Cleveland Road
Barnes
London
SW13 0AA

8 October 1998

Dear Mr Wendlow,

Further to your letter of 1 October, membership of the
Garrick Club is by invitation rather than application. A
candidate must be proposed and seconded by existing
members to whom he is well known and we currently
have a waiting list of approximately eight years.

The current annual subscription is £846.84 with an initial
joining fee of the same amount.

Yours sincerely,

Martin Harvey
Secretary

Oscar Wendlow
'Portrait Painter To The Stars'
Cleveland Road, Barnes,
London SW13 0AA

Martin Harvey
Secretary's Office
The Garrick Club
15, Garrick Street
London WC2E 9AY   22nd October 1998

Dear Martin,

EIGHT YEARS! I hope that's a printing error! Ha, ha! Seriously though,
you say in your letter that I would need to be proposed and seconded by
two existing members. The problem is I don't know any! Would you be
so kind as to send me the names and addresses of two 'respected' (and
hopefully famous!) members who could propose me? Also, would you be
interested in seeing some photos of my paintings to prove I am a REAL
artist and not just some ponce trying to 'worm his way in'?

I look forward to hearing from you.

Yours sincerely,

Ocar Wendlow

PS   I am enclosing £20 in the hope that it might speed things up a bit,
      say, one year instead of eight?

With the Secretary's Compliments.

Garrick Club
15, Garrick Street,
London. WC2E 9AY

LONDON
26.10.98
WC2

GREAT BRITAIN ✦ 026 POSTAGE PAID
PB714960

O Wendlow Esq
'Portrait Painter To The Stars'
Cleveland Road
Barnes
London SW13 OAA

Oscar Wendlow
'Portrait Painter To The Stars'
Cleveland Road, Barnes,
London SW13 0AA

Martin Harvey
Secretary's Office
The Garrick Club
15 Garrick Street
London WC2E 9AY   4th November 1998

Dear Martin,

A few days ago I received an envelope from you containing a twenty pound note and a business card and NOTHING ELSE! NO APPLICATION FORM and NO NAMES OF NOMINEES! Don't worry, I understand! You were obviously having 'one of those days'. If you were a woman you could blame it on PMT Ha, ha! I find the older I get the more forgetful I am too. It's shocking! I recently posted an envelope that was COMPLETELY EMPTY and on another occasion I wrote two letters and addressed two envelopes then put the wrong letters in the envelopes and posted them! The following day I received two puzzled phone calls Ha, ha! Don't worry about it! You are probably a very busy man.

Anyway, I thought it would simplify things if I were to 'pop' into the club personally. Then you could give me the appropriate 'info' and possibly show me around! I'm going to be in your 'neck of the woods' next Thursday, the 12th November. So unless I hear from you in the meantime I will 'drop in' at the Garrick about 2.00 'ish'. (Incidentally, I was passing the club the other day and I thought it looked very grubby. With those huge membership fees I thought the least you could do is keep the place looking smart!) (Don't worry, I still want to join!)

I look forward to meeting you next Friday. Cheers!

Yours Sincerely,

Ocar Wendlow

PS   Remind me to ask you if the club has a Jacuzzi.

PPS   Could my other 'alf become a joint member?

Secretary's Office .

Telephone:
0171-836 1737

O Wendlow Esq
 Cleveland Road
Barnes
London   SW13 0AA

Garrick Club,
Garrick Street,
WC2E 9AY.

10 November 1998

Dear Sir,

As explained in my previous letter, membership of the Garrick Club is by invitation, not application. Potential candidates must be proposed and seconded by members of at least three years' standing to whom the candidate is well known. As such, any nomination is in the hands of the member and I am therefore unable to offer any help.

I can add nothing further to the information already given and there is, therefore, no purpose to be served by you calling into the Club.

Yours faithfully,

Martin Harvey
Secretary

Oscar Wendlow
'Portrait Painter To The Stars'
Cleveland Road, Barnes,
London SW13 0AA

HRH Queen Elizabeth
Buckingham Palace
London SW1A 1AA   25th September 1998

Dear Ma'am,

My wife and I have been discussing the ongoing Prince Edward – Sophie Rhys-Jones
situation at some length, and finally felt compelled to put pen to paper.

Forgive me for poking my nose into your private family affairs but what I am about to
say has to be said; EDWARD HAS GOT TO STOP SITTING ON THE FENCE!

It's not fair to keep stringing Sophie along like this. She deserves better! He has got to
pull his finger out and 'pop the question' or, alternatively, set her free! As my wife,
Joyce said, 'She's not getting any younger'. She should be married now and popping
sprogs, (having children) not sitting around twiddling her thumbs while Edward
ponces about in front of a TV camera. IT'S NOT FAIR! She's a lovely girl. He's
wasting her best years.

Can't you or Prince Philip have a quiet word with him? LET'S FACE IT , 'people are
talking' and what they are saying is not very pleasant. All he has to do to dispel the
rumours about Sophie being a 'cover' is pop the question! Then BINGO , all the
doubts about his manhood will disappear.

Forgive my impertinence Ma'am but I thought you might like to know the feeling 'on
the ground'. I look forward to hearing from you and hope this situation can be quickly
resolved.

We want to see Edward and Sophie walking up the aisle!

Yours sincerely from a true blue
Tory royalist and fellow parent,

Ocar Wendlow

BALMORAL CASTLE

29th September, 1998

Dear Mr. Wendlow,

The Queen has asked me to thank you for your letter of 25th September, and to say that the views you express about Prince Edward and Miss Sophie Rhys-Jones have been noted.

Yours sincerely

MRS. DEBORAH BEAN
Chief Correspondence Officer

Oscar Wendlow, Esq.

HRH Prince Edward
Buckingham Palace
London SW1A 1AA   1st October 1998

Dear Sir,

I have just received a very nice letter from H.R.H. The Queen (your mother) at Balmoral, thanking me for the comments I made in a recent letter to her about your on-going relationship with Sophie Rhys-Jones.

Forgive me for going 'behind your back' but I felt the Queen should be made aware of the feeling 'on the street'. I told her that you have got to STOP SITTING ON THE FENCE! and POP THE QUESTION! Let's face it, you're beginning to make Sophie look an idiot, keeping her hanging on like this. IT'S NOT FAIR. She's a lovely girl! What's the problem?

And, I'm sorry but it has to be said; people are beginning to say unkind things about the 'cut of your gib'. 'PRINCE EDWARD IS NOT A POOF!' I say, but to be honest sir, the longer this drags on the more hollow my assertions sound.

So, if when your mother returns from Balmoral she takes you to one side and repeats what I've just said don't be surprised. I make no apologies for interfering. If I can be the 'catalyst' that brings this unsatisfactory situation to a long overdue and joyful conclusion I will be a happy man.

Nothing would give me and my other 'alf greater pleasure than seeing you and Sophie skipping up the aisle! Who knows, we might even be there in person (hint! hint! ha, ha!) Come on sir, GO FOR IT!

I was sorry to miss your recent T.V. series on the Thames. Will it be repeated? I look forward to hearing from you.

Yours sincerely,

Oscar Wendlow

58

From: Lieutenant Colonel Sean O'Dwyer, LVO

BUCKINGHAM PALACE

6th October, 1998

Dear Mr Wendlow,

The Prince Edward has asked me to acknowledge your letter of 1st October 1998 concerning his relationship with Miss Rhys-Jones.

I would have thought that this relationship was an entirely private matter between the two individuals concerned and had nothing to do with you or indeed me. If Miss Rhys-Jones does not like the situation she can always walk away from it. Putting pressure on either of them will not help.

I believe that the TV series that you missed was 'Crown and Country' - six half hour programmes on various aspects of London. They may be shown on the History Channel in the near future and it is up to Carlton whether they repeat - let us hope so.

Yours sincerely,

Sean O'Dwyer.

Private Secretary to HRH The Prince Edward, CVO

Oscar Wendlow Esq

London SW1A 1AA

Oscar Wendlow
'Portrait Painter To The Stars'
Cleveland Road, Barnes,
London SW13 0AA

Lt. Col. Sean O Dwyer, LVO
Buckingham Palace
London SW1A 1AA   22nd October 1998

Dear Sean,

Thank you for your letter of 6th October 1998. YOU'RE RIGHT! Edward and Sophie's relationship is a private matter and has nothing to do with the likes of you and me. However, I AM A ROYALIST and as such I want to see the royals happily married and popping sprogs (having children) NOT poncing about in front of TV cameras trying to be showbiz 'personalities'.

Lets face it, Sean, this courtship has been going on for at least five years. Why so long? What's the problem? If they're not going to get 'hitched' they should 'call it a day' and stop wasting everybody's time. This country NEEDS a royal wedding! It would CHEER US UP!

As you can see from my heading I 'dabble in oils'. I am planning to write to Edward to ask if he would be interested in me painting a double portrait (a double-whammy ha,ha!) of him and Sophie in a loving pose. In the event of a happy announcement they could then release the picture to the press.

The painting would require about half a dozen 'sittings'. Could you let me know if Edward would be interested or should I write to him personally?

Also, as I have taken such an interest in this case, would there be any chance of a couple of invitations to the wedding? (grovel! grovel! Ha, ha!)

I look forward to hearing from you.

Yours sincerely,

Oscar Wendlow

I am enclosing £5 to cover your expenses

From: Lieutenant Colonel Sean O'Dwyer, LVO

BUCKINGHAM PALACE

2nd November, 1998

Dear Mr Wendlow,

Thank you for your letter of the 22nd November in which you ask if you might paint a portrait of The Prince Edward and Miss Rhys-Jones.

Your thought is appreciated, but I have to inform you that this is something that His Royal Highness does not wish to pursue. I am sorry to disappoint you.

Thank you for enclosing £5 to cover expenses, but this is quite unnecessary and I am returning it to you.

Yours sincerely,

Sean O'Dwyer.

Private Secretary to HRH The Prince Edward, CVO

Oscar Wendlow Esq

London SW1A 1AA

Oscar Wendlow
'Portrait Painter To The Stars'
Cleveland Road, Barnes,
London SW13 0AA

Maggie Koumi
Hello! Limited
Wellington House
69-71 Upper Ground
London SE1 9PQ   30th September 1998

Dear Maggie Koumi,

I am currently putting together an exhibition of portraits of famous 'personalities' to be titled 'BRITISH SUPERSTARS OF THE ARTS AND CULTURE AND POP MUSIC IN BRITAIN AT THE REAR END OF THE NINETIES', which will be held as part of the Millennium celebrations. I had talks with Peter Mandelson about the Millennium Dome in Greenwich as a possible venue but both he and Sir Richard Rogers felt my work was more suited to a 'conventional' west end gallery like Waddingtons and I agree with them. I have since exchanged letters with Leslie Waddington who is ' gagging' to show my work at his Cork St gallery. This now looks like the most probably venue.

The exhibition will be held next summer and needless to say, the private view will be a 'star studded' affair. Would Hello! be interested in covering the event? There will be a VERITABLE PLETHORA of ' personalities' from the worlds of pop, TV, Politics and the Media etc.

I also wondered if you might be interested in doing a feature on me in my home. I am expecting to receive an honour in Tony Blair's new year list so a feature on me next year could tie in quite nicely.

I look forward to hearing from you.

Yours,

Ocar Wendlow

PS I have done a portrait of Diana Princess of Wales (looking sad) of which I am particularly proud. Perhaps you could use it for a front cover?

● HELLO LIMITED, Wellington House, 69-71 Upper Ground, London SE1 9PQ Telephone: 0171-667 8700 ●
Fax: 0171-667 8716

6 October 1998

Oscar Wendlow
   Cleveland Road
Barnes
LONDON
SW13 0AA

Dear Mr Wendlow

Thank you for your letter.

The magazine is normally invited to most events where there are
celebrities - and we do most certainly get invited to nearly all the art
exhibitions.

We don't use illustrations or paintings in our magazine unless there is
a news story surrounding them and we certainly wouldn't use a
painting as our cover - but thank you very much for your offer.

We will of course be most interested to see your exhibition at the Cork
Street gallery and I wish you lots of success.

Best wishes

Yours sincerely

Maggie Koumi
EDITOR

● Registered in England, No: 2210024 Registered address: Wellington House, 69-71 Upper Ground, London SE1 9PQ ●

Oscar Wendlow
'Portrait Painter To The Stars'
Cleveland Road, Barnes,
London SW13 0AA

Maggie Kouni,
Hello! Magazine,
Wellington House,
69-71 Upper Ground
London SE1 9PQ   22nd October 1998

Dear Maggie,

Thank you for your letter of 6th October regarding my 'upcoming' show at Waddingtons. I am happy to confirm that you will be receiving invitations nearer the time.

JUST ONE THING! What is the 'deal' moneywise? i.e. Who pays whom? Are we expected to 'cough up' because you are promoting the exhibition? OR do you pay us because you are getting loads of photo's of showbiz personalities to fill your magazine? I know its not nice to talk about money when (lets face it) we're all scratching each others backs, and I don't want to seem 'mercenary'. However it doesn't seem 'right' that Hello! Should get loads of photos of celebrities 'buckshee', especially when 10% of the proceeds of the show are going to a charity (Retired Taxi Drivers Fund) What do you think?

Incidentally, I have received a very nice letter from Lt. Col. Sean O'Dwyer, private secretary to HRH Prince Edward and I am hoping to confirm the presence of the Prince and Miss Sophie Rhys Jones at the opening of my exhibition, shortly. Fingers crossed!

I look forward to hearing your response to my query.

Yours Sincerely,

Oscar Wendlow

● HELLO LIMITED, Wellington House, 69-71 Upper Ground, London SE1 9PQ Telephone: 0171-667 8700 ●
Fax: 0171-667 8716

29 October 1998

Oscar Wendlow
  Cleveland Road
Barnes
LONDON
SW13 0AA

Dear Oscar

Thank you for your letter but I am not quite sure I understand it!

No, of course you wouldn't have to pay us if we were to use any
photographs from your exhibition. Neither would we pay you as we
have to pay the photographers who took the photographs.

I wish you a very successful day.

Best wishes

Yours sincerely

Maggie Koumi
EDITOR

● Registered in England, No: 2210024 Registered address: Wellington House, 69-71 Upper Ground, London SE1 9PQ ●

Oscar Wendlow
'Portrait Painter To The Stars'
Cleveland Road, Barnes,
London SW13 0AA

Maggie Kouni,
Hello! Magazine,
Wellington House,
69-71 Upper Ground,
London SE1 9PQ   4th November 1998

Dear Maggie,

Thank you for your letter of 29th October in response to my query about 'who pays whom'. I think we understand each other. However, I do hope that nearer the time Hello! might consider making a small donation to the Retired Taxi Drivers Fund (a very worthy charity I am sure you will agree).

As my exhibition of portraits next summer will be my 'BIG LAUNCH' into the London art world (tremble, tremble, Ha, ha!) it is very important to me that it goes SMOOTHLY. Therefore, I would just like to clear up one last point. Whenever I have seen members of the 'paparazzi' either on TV or on the streets of London they have usually looked quite scruffy and 'unkempt'. As you know I am expecting 'Royalty' at my opening, not to mention numerous 'celebrities' who will be looking smart and 'glamorous' for the occasion. What worries me is the thought of your photographers turning up looking dirty and unshaven etc. and 'lowering the tone' of the evening.

Can you give me your personal assurance that your 'snappers' will look 'snappy'? Ha, ha! It would be a great shame if the evening was spoiled by a few 'slobs'. Many Thanks.

Yours sincerely,

Ocar Wendlow

PS   I am enclosing £5 to cover your admin. costs. Cheers!

● HELLO LIMITED, Wellington House, 69-71 Upper Ground, London SE1 9PQ Telephone: 0171-667 8700 ●
Fax: 0171-667 8716

10 November 1998

REGISTERED POST
Mr Oscar Wendlow
  Cleveland Road
Barnes
LONDON
SW13 0AA

Dear Mr Wendlow

Thank you for your letter.

Your comments have been noted and I return your £5 as we do not
charge for administration costs.

Best wishes

Yours sincerely

Maggie Koumi
EDITOR

● Registered in England, No: 2210024 Registered address: Wellington House, 69-71 Upper Ground, London SE1 9PQ ●

Oscar Wendlow
'Portrait Painter To The Stars'
Cleveland Road, Barnes,
London SW13 0AA

Sir Paul Condon
New Scotland Yard
Broadway
London SW1 H0BG   25th September 1998

Dear Sir,

I am writing to you as a London cab driver of some 22 years experience to say that I am absolutely FED UP with cyclists using the designated 'bus and taxi' lanes. I can't tell you how many 'near-misses' I have had in recent months because I have lost count. It's these young messengers, they are kamikaze maniacs. They think they own the road, all dressed up in their fancy gear! They swerve in front of you without any warning and just laugh or give you the 'two fingers up' if you hoot at them (or one finger as seems to be the current trend).

With all due respect I don't think your 'boys in blue' are doing enough to stamp out their reckless behaviour. Something has got to be done and NOW!

Firstly I would like to suggest immunity from prosecution for any cab driver who is in collision with a cyclist. That way, when they 'cut us up' we could legally pursue them, knock them off their bikes then continue about our business, providing a service to the general public.

Alternatively, I suggest a system of razor sharp spikes connected to some form of bicycle detector. Whenever the detector is activated the spikes would shoot up out of the road puncturing the bicycle tyres and tripping the cyclist up. THAT WOULD GIVE THEM SOMETHING TO THINK ABOUT!

This solution may seem a bit extreme but I feel something radical has to be done before the highways and byways of London end up completely at the mercy of these lycra loonies.

I look forward to hearing your plan of action!

Yours sincerely,

Ocar Wendlow

Date: 30th September 1998

METROPOLITAN POLICE

Mr O Wendlow
 Cleveland Road
Barnes
SW13 OAA

METROPOLITAN POLICE SERVICE

24 Hour Response & Trafffic
Room 1011
New Scotland Yard
Broadway
London SW1H OBG
Tel: 0171-230-3035
Fax: 0171-230-3747

Dear Mr Wendlow,

Thank you for your letter addressed to the Commissioner, Sir Paul Condon.

I note your comments and appreciate that the inconsiderate actions of some road users inconveniences many.

Police seek to address such problems within the constraints imposed by the need to prioritise demands, given our finite resources.

Thank you for taking the trouble to write.

Yours sincerely

Stephen Zorab
Inspector
sz/wendlow

31st October 1997

John Holroyd, Esq.,
10, Downing Street,
London,
SW1A.

Dear Mr. Holroyd,

I would like to nominate someone for a mention in your next honours list. Would you be so kind as to send me a nomination form?

Yours sincerely,

Oscar Wendlow

HONOURS NOMINATION FORM

GENERAL INFORMATION

The Prime Minister welcomes honours nominations from members of the public.

He wants his list to be representative of society as a whole - men and women from all walks of life including those from the ethnic communities.

There are only 1,000 awards in each Prime Minister's Honours List, so only those who have given *exceptional service* are likely to succeed. (This does not mean that the contributions of other candidates go unappreciated or unnoticed.)

You may submit a nomination at any time. Receipt of your Nomination Form will be acknowledged within 28 days, but it is not possible to provide any further information, or progress reports, on your nomination.

QUESTIONS COMMONLY ASKED ABOUT HONOURS

1) *Should I tell the person I have nominated them?*
No. It is not fair to raise a nominee's expectations in case they are disappointed.

2) *Do I have to say what sort of honour I think is due?*
No. We will do that for you.

3) *How long will the process take?*
It will take a minimum of six months to deal with an application in readiness for the New Year or the Birthday (June) Honours Lists, and is more likely to take 12-18 months for even a strong candidate to succeed, given the high level of competition.

4) *May I nominate someone who is no longer involved in the activity(ies) I wish to see recognised?*
Yes, but only if they ceased their involvement within the past six months. (See note 9 overleaf.)

5) *How will I know if my nomination is successful?*
If your nominee is successful his or her name will appear in the list published in the national newspapers at the New Year or on The Queen's Birthday (June).

6) *If my nomination is not successful, may I re-nominate?*
Yes, provided the person nominated is still engaged in the work which prompted you to nominate in the first place. We suggest you do not re-nominate until 18 months have elapsed since the original nomination was made.

HONOURS NOMINATION FORM

PLEASE USE BLOCK CAPITALS (PREFERABLY USING BLACK INK) OR TYPESCRIPT WHEN COMPLETING THIS FORM AND AVOID ABBREVIATIONS WHERE POSSIBLE. YOU MUST COMPLETE SECTIONS 1-6 ON THIS FORM OR WE WILL BE UNABLE TO CONSIDER YOUR NOMINEE.

1. YOUR NAME AND ADDRESS

OSCAR WENDLOW,
CLEVELAND ROAD,
LONDON SW13 0AA.

Your telephone number (including area code): 0181-876-5911

2. NOMINEE'S FULL NAME AND ADDRESS

OSCAR ALBERT UNWIN WENDLOW

'AS ABOVE'

3. NOMINEE'S DATE OF BIRTH (or approximate age) 53

4. NOMINEE'S NATIONALITY: BRITISH (TO THE CORE)

5. THE RECOMMENDATION   Give full details of the ACHIEVEMENTS of your nominee and how he or she has contributed personally to the activities for which an honour is recommended. Use a continuation sheet if necessary.

* I AM VERY HONEST. WHEN A CUSTOMER LEFT HER HANDBAG CONTAINING £2,400 CASH IN THE BACK OF MY CAB I TRACED HER AND RETURNED IT.

* I STARTED A NEIGHBOURHOOD WATCH SCHEME WHICH WAS A GREAT SUCCESS FOR A WHILE.

* I AM A GOOD NEIGHBOUR AND HAVE BEEN A ROCK (HER WORD) TO MARGARET (NEXT-DOOR-BUT-ONE) SINCE HER HUSBAND, GORDON PASSED ON (CANCER)

* I ALWAYS TRY TO BRIGHTEN MY CUSTOMERS DAY WITH A SMILE AND A JOKE (I CAN'T STAND MOANERS)

* I AM A GOOD HUSBAND AND FATHER (NOT THAT I GET ANY THANKS FOR IT!)

* I'VE HAD TWO OF MY POEMS PUBLISHED IN 'CAB DRIVER'

Form Continued Overleaf

Detach Here

6. BACKGROUND Give full details of POST(S) HELD, PAID or VOLUNTARY, with dates, and describe the work of the nominee and the activities for which an honour is recommended. Use a continuation sheet if necessary.

* 1955: FIRST JOB (WEEKENDS). HELPING RAT CATCHER AT THAMES ST. SEWAGE WORKS, GREENWICH. PAID A 'BOB' A DAY. (SEEMED LIKE RICHES THEN!)

* 1957: SECOND JOB (WEEKENDS) UNITED DAIRIES DEPOT, EDWARD ST. DEPTFORD. MUCKING-OUT STABLES (PHEW, WHAT A PONG!)

* 1957: JOINED KING WILLIAM BOYS CLUB, GREENWICH. AMATEUR BOXER FOR SIX YEARS. WON THIRTEEN TROPHIES.

* 1958: LEFT SCHOOL. DAD GOT ME APPRENTICESHIP AT NEWLINE PRINTERS, NEW CROSS. BECAME QUALIFIED PRINTER/ENGRAVER.

* 1966: MOVED TO TUDOR ENGRAVING, TOOTING.

* 1969: MOVED TO ALPHAPRINT LTD. WIMBLEDON.

* 1971: STARTED DOING 'THE KNOWLEDGE'.

* 1975: GOT MY BADGE. STARTED CABBING.

* ALWAYS VERY INTERESTED IN 'THE ARTS'.

* 1995: TOOK UP PAINTING EVENING CLASSES (DUCK TO WATER!)

* 1997-98: ATTEMPTING TO GET MAJOR EXHIBITION OF PAINTINGS OF BRITISH PERSONALITIES OFF GROUND AS PART OF THE MILLENIUM CELEBRATIONS.

* DO TAXI DRIVERS CHARITY FUN-RUN TO BRIGHTON EVERY YEAR.

* MAKE REGULAR CONTRIBUTIONS TO NSPCC.

* ALWAYS GIVE TO CHARITY COLLECTORS IN THE STREET.

* A NEIGHBOUR RECENTLY DESCRIBED ME AS A 'ROCK'. PEOPLE ALWAYS KNOW THEY CAN COME TO ME WITH A PROBLEM. I'M A SORT OF LIFE-LONG VOLUNTARY UNPAID COUNSELLOR + GOOD SAMARITAN.

Remember to attach your 2 (or more) co-sponsors letters of support.
Or tick this box to indicate that these will be sent separately. ☐

RETURN THIS FORM TO:

The Nominations Unit
Honours Secretariat
10 Downing Street
LONDON SW1A 2AA

Telephone number: 0171-210 5071/5065

Facsimile number: 0171-210 5046

Due to the large number of nominations received we cannot respond to enquires about the progress of particular cases.

GENERAL ENQUIRES about the honours system should be made to the Ceremonial Officer, Cabinet Office, 53 Parliament Street, London SW1A 2NG.

To The Nominations Secretariat
Honours Unit   26 September 1998
10, Downing Street
London SW1A 2AA

To Sir,
My mate Ozzie has asked me to write a letter backing up the honour which it is applied for. Yer I think he deserves one Why not? I don't reckon they should be just for "toffs" and the higher ups of society Why not make them give them also to the ~~higher~~ ordinary working man? Hes always been a good mate and we been mates for long-long time and good mates aswell and I can always relly on him He told me to tell about the charity work he done he told good on him. He said he done a Lot good an him. Yer I reckon he deserves an honour why not? Hes always been a good mate. Yer definitely give him an honour. Good Luck. The end.

Be Lucky! Ron Loxton.

Ron Loxton
30 Ravenna Crescent
Battersea
London SW1A 2AA

74

Violet Wendlow
c/o   Cleveland Road
Barnes
SW13 0AA

24th September 1998

To whom it may concern,

This is a letter of support for my son, Oscar's application for an honour. If anyone deserves an honour he does. He's a 'super chap'. A wonderful son, husband and father. I often think his wife and children don't appreciate him enough, they take him 'for granted' but he never complains. He's worked hard all his life and done very well for himself. He's very generous and always giving money to charities and he's a very good neighbour and friend. He keeps an eye on the old folk in his road and makes sure they are warm enough in winter. Nothing is 'too much trouble'. He loves to help people. They take advantage of his sometimes because he's so kind and generous. He is also a talented artist and very interested in literature, poetry and all things 'cultural'. If you counted up all the money he has given to charities over the years it would be a FORTUNE, but he doesn't care. He doesn't want to be a millionaire. I hope you give him an honour. If you don't it will be a travesty.

Yours sincerely,

CABINET OFFICE

CEREMONIAL BRANCH

Nominations Unit

Ashley House • 2 Monck Street • London SW1P 2BQ
TELEPHONE: 0171-276 2779 • FAX: 0171-276 2766

DATE • 02 October 1998

OUR REFERENCE •

YOUR REFERENCE •

Oscar A U Wendlow Esq
Cleveland Road
London SW13 0AA

Dear Mr Wendlow

Thank you for returning your completed nomination form and letters of support recommending yourself for an Honour.

I am sorry to have to tell you that it will not be possible to consider you for an Honour as awards are to recognise meritorious service to the community or contribution to public life in this country. I should also explain that it is not usual for the Prime Minister to recommend Honours for anyone on the basis of a self nomination.

I regret sending this disappointing reply.

Yours sincerely

Vikki Martin
Case Officer

Oscar Wendlow
'Portrait Painter To The Stars'
Cleveland Road, Barnes,
London SW13 0AA

Ms Vikki Martin,   5th October 1998
Nominations Unit,
Ashley House,
2, Monck Street,
London SW1P 2BQ

Dear Vikki Martin,

I have just received your letter and I must admit I am GUTTED! You say an Honour
is an award to recognise 'meritorious service to the community or contributions to
public life in this country'.

I have been a London cab driver for 23 YEARS! WHAT IS THAT if it is not service
to the community and a contribution to public life? Imagine London WITHOUT cabs!
It would be CHAOS! How would people like YOU get to work?

You also say the Prime Minister doesn't recommend Honours for anyone on the basis
of a 'self-nomination'. But who is better qualified to nominate me than ME? Only I
know how much good I've done and how much sunshine I bring into my customers
lives! Only I know how much money I've given to charities! (I don't go around
shouting about it from the rooftops!) Only I know what a good neighbour, husband
and father I am etc. etc.!

ALSO, what about all the people I have told I'm getting an Honour? What do I say to
them?

I feel I have been unfairly judged and hope you will RECONSIDER my nomination
with a bit more thought. DON'T BE SO HASTY!

Yours in anticipation of good news,

Ocar Wendlow

PS   What about that policeman who got an Honour for standing outside
        number ten? I don't think HE did much good for public life in this
        country, do you Vikki?

PPS   Please accept the enclosed £50 as a personal gift.

CABINET OFFICE

CEREMONIAL BRANCH

Nominations Unit

Ashley House • 2 Monck Street • London SW1P 2BQ
TELEPHONE: 0171-276 0000 • FAX: 0171-276 2766

DATE • 15 October 1998

OUR REFERENCE •

YOUR REFERENCE •

Oscar Wendlow Esq
  Cleveland Road
Barnes
London
SW13 OAA

Dear Mr Wendlow

I have seen your letter to Miss Martin, asking to be reconsidered for an Honour.

I understand your disappointment in not being considered for an award but as Miss Martin explained in her letter of 2 October 1998, it is customary for nominations to carry some impartial support. Preferably the nominator should be someone other than the individual concerned, but self nomination is not unknown, though it is not encouraged and is not of itself sufficient. We also require some collateral comment sent to us directly (i.e. not via the self nominator).

As you will see from the Nomination Form (enclosed) the award of an honours is competitive - there are far more honours nominations than places available. This does not mean that services to the community of the sort you mention are not appreciated, but it is the result of the appraisal process. For the present, the contribution you have made to the Taxi industry and to your local community is being appraised.

I am returning the £50 personal gift that you sent to Miss Martin. We never accept such payments. I would be grateful if you would return the enclosed acknowledgement slip.

Yours Sincerely

Lesley Watling

Lesley Watling

Oscar Wendlow
'Portrait Painter To The Stars'
Cleveland Road, Barnes,
London SW13 0AA

Dr Prakash   4th October 1998
c/o Surgical Advisory Service,
82, Harley Street,
London W1N 1AE

Dear Dr Prakash,

My spies tell me that you are THE person to speak to when it comes to surgical hair implants. Due to a 'major cultural event' I am organising, I am going to be spending a lot of time in the public eye from next summer (TV, newspapers, magazine features, etc.) As you know cameras are not 'kind' to big, shiny foreheads so I have been seriously considering doing something about my receding hairline.

In recent years I have grown an abundance of hair on my shoulders, back and lower back (arse). Would it be possible to transplant some of this hair onto my head? I would naturally prefer to use my own hair rather than someone else's.

Also, I would want the treatment to be subtle. I don't want to look like Elton John! If you could drop me a line at the above I would be most appreciative.

It has just occurred to me that it might be a good idea to film the process as a TV documentary! What do you think?

I look forward to hearing from you.

Yours sincerely,

Oscar Wendlow

Oscar Wendlow
'Portrait Painter To The Stars'
Cleveland Road, Barnes,
London SW13 0AA

Mr Mathew Robinson
Eastenders
BBC Elstree Centre
Clarendon Road
Boreham Wood
HERTS WD6 1JF
                                                                    23rd October 1998

Dear Mr Robinson,

My other 'alf and I are big fans of Eastenders and I happen to be a GENUINE 'eastender'
myself being born and brought up in Greenwich and Deptford.

I am writing to ask if you would consider having a 'non-professional' actor on the show? If so
I would be very interested in having 'a bash'. I haven't had any training as an actor but I have
been to the 'UNIVERSITY OF LIFE' which is probably more important (in the long run). I
can do quite good impressions:

JAMES CAGNEY-   You durdy raat!
MAX BYGRAVES-   I wanna tell you a stawry!
TOMMY COOPER-   Just like that! Not like that! Like that! Ha, ha!
BRUCE FORSYTH-   Good game! Good game!

I am a cab driver so I have lots of opportunities to study 'characters'. I also paint (portraits of
celebrities), so I am definitely 'creative' and 'artistic'. TO BE HONEST driving a cab doesn't
'FULFILL' me. I need something else in life and I think acting could be IT.

I have thought about a role for me in the show. Here is my idea:

Grant and Phil are walking through the market when a taxi cab (me) drives past. I slam on the
brakes and say 'Oi!'. Grant and Phil walk over and I say 'you look like the Mitchell brothers'.
They say 'What's it to you?' and I say 'I'm your long-lost uncle Oscar. I ain't seen you since
you was nippers!' They say 'We didn't know we 'ad an uncle!' Then they invite me into the
'Vic' for a drink.

Peggy (Barbara Windsor) is surprised to see me and says 'Cor Blimey, its you!' and we
exchange a look which indicates (to the viewers) that we were once MORE than just brother
and sister-in-law. We all have a few drinks then I (foolishly) get in my cab to drive home. I
have an accident, get my legs smashed up and end up wheelchair-bound. Grant feels guilty
and invites me to live at the 'Vic'. Peggy and I fall in love, my legs get better and I take over
the pub and run it for years to come.

What do you think? As you can see, I would be interested in contributing to the scripts as
well.

I will be very grateful if you consider me for Eastenders and look forward to hearing from
you. I definitely think my future is in acting.

Yours in anticipation,

Oscar Wendlow

Oscar Wendlow
  Cleveland Road
Barnes
London
SW13 0AA

26th October 1998

Dear Mr Wendlow

Thank you for your letter and storyline suggestion for EastEnders, and your enquiry about a possible role in the programme.

As I am sure you'll appreciate we receive many storyline ideas from viewers for our characters, but the commissioning process for storylines does not work in this way. Creating stories for EastEnders in which traditionally ten or more stories run at any given time, is an enormous and complex process which can take anything between one and three years to develop. Storyliners, Producers, Script Editors and Writers are involved since the logistical elements of change in terms of cast and production constantly impinge. For a wide variety of editorial, legal, copyright and other reasons we cannot accept storylines from viewers whatever their merit. We have a very large team of commissioned writers and storyliners.

We also receive numerous letters from people wanting to appear in the programme. It is EastEnders policy only to employ artists who can provide evidence of previous acting experience in television or theatre. All of our casting is carried out by our casting advisor, who contacts artists through agencies. If you have not already done so, it would be advisable to register with an actors' agency. We are not able to recommend specific agencies, as it would not be ethical to do so. However, you can find the details for many reputable agents listed in the publication entitled "Contacts", which you should be able to purchase from any good book shop and you could also try your local library who should have a copy. Alternatively, you could contact Equity direct for advice.

We do, however, thank you for your interest and we hope you continue to watch and enjoy EastEnders.

Yours sincerely

Matthew Robinson
Executive Producer
EastEnders

B B C Production

British Broadcasting Corporation Elstree Centre Clarendon Road Borehamwood Herts WD6 1JF
Telephone 0181 228 7777 Fax 0181 228 8670

1

Oscar Wendlow
'Portrait Painter To The Stars'
Cleveland Road, Barnes,
London SW13 0AA

Barbara Windsor,
Eastenders,
BBC Elstree Centre,
Clarendon Road
Boreham Wood
HERTS WD6 1JF   4th November 1998

Dear Barbara Windsor,

My other 'alf and I have been HUGE fans of yours for many years and we
were CHUFFED TO BITS when you joined the cast of 'Eastenders'. We think
you are excellent as Peggy and are BIG fans of the show. In fact, I am such a
big fan that I want to be IN it! Ha, ha!

To that end I am enclosing a copy of a letter I recently sent to your executive
producer, Mathew Robinson. He sent me a 'disappointing' reply, telling me
that you never consider actors without 'experience'. That seems a bit
STRANGE. If the show is supposed to be 'REALISTIC' surely you would
want to employ REAL eastenders! Don't you agree? I wondered if you could
have a word in his 'shell-like' and ask him to 'reconsider'.

It's true I haven't had any acting experience but how am I going to get any if
people like Mathew don't give me a break?! It would certainly be an honour
to work with you, Barbara, and I'm sure we would have a great 'sexual
chemistry' as they say. Ha, ha! I must say I am not at all happy about your
engagement to Frank Butcher. I think you're going to regret that! Never mind,
if I join the show maybe the scriptwriters could kill him off! Ha, ha!

I hope you will do what you can to help a fellow cockney who's got a NOT
INCONSIDERABLE amount of talent and LOADS of enthusiasm!

Keep up the good work and is there any chance of a signed photo?

Yours sincerely, your cockney mate,

Oscar Wendlow

BARBARA WINDSOR

Oscar Wendlow,
  Cleveland Road,
Barnes,
London. SW13 0AA.

30 December, 1998

Dear Oscar,

Barbara Windsor has asked me to write and thank you for your letter
dated 4 November and I apologise for the delay in replying.

As Mathew Robinson said, the EastEnders cast are trained actors
with experience - but most of them are real EastEnders and that's
why the show is so realistic. If you seriously want to pursue an
acting career, it may be worth attending drama classes or
alternatively look at joining an extras agency and try for work as
a background artist.

Barbara thanks you for your lovely comments about her performance
as Peggy. It's a role she loves playing.

She sends her warmest regards and all good wishes for 1999.

Best wishes,

Yvonne I'Anson,
P.A. to Barbara Windsor.

Oscar Wendlow
'Portrait Painter To The Stars'
Cleveland Road, Barnes,
London SW13 0AA

Michael Winner
(Restaurant Critic)   23rd October 1998
The Sunday Times,
1, Virginia St.
London E1 9BD

Dear Mr Winner,

My spies tell me that you are now a top restaurant critic and a regular contributor to the Sunday Times. If so you could be just the person I'm looking for!

My wife and I have recently come up with a business idea which we think could be a great success.

You know what it's like when you are walking along the street and you just fancy a Mars bar or a packet of crisps or a nice cold can of Coke but there aren't any shops in the immediate vicinity or they are the wrong type of shops. DING, DONG! DING, DONG! That's where <u>we</u> come in.

A neighbour of ours has an 'E' reg ice cream van for sale and has just accepted our offer of £3,800 for it. We intend to convert it into a mobile shop serving snacks, meat pies, hot and cold drinks and GOURMET SANDWICHES! The idea is that people will 'hail' the van the way you would 'hail' a taxi and for this reason we have come up with the name 'TAXISNAX'. I would 'pull over' to the side of the road and my wife, Joyce would serve the customer (while I keep my eyes open for members of the local constabulary ha, ha!)

Joyce is very keen to serve high class 'nouvelle cuisine' sandwiches: cream cheese and fig, smoked ham and starfruit, salami and kiwi fruit, smoked turkey and peach etc.

That's where <u>you</u> come in! When the van is ready for launch (about three months) it would be a big help to have some publicity and press coverage. We wondered if you would like to come to Barnes to sample Joyce's wares and do a feature on us? If you like her sandwiches as much as I do perhaps we could write 'As recommended by Michael Winner of the Sunday Times' on the back of the van!

We do hope you will be interested and help us get our venture off the ground. Perhaps you would like to become a shareholder?

We look forward to hearing from you.

Yours expectantly,

Oscar Wendlow

SCIMITAR FILMS LTD.

Directors: Michael Winner M.A. (CANTAB), *John Fraser M.A.* (OXON), *M. Phil.*

Den Oscar

Thank you for writing to me. Your views about food-service-restaurants are very interesting.

I have passed your letter on to the Editor of the Style Section of The Sunday Times because it seems very suitable for publication. They may want to cut it a bit, I hope they will use it. The Style editorial people select the letters!

Thanks again,

Good Luck and God Bless ....

MICHAEL WINNER

27.10.98

Mr Duncan Clegg
119 Albert St.
London NW1 7NB

24th September 1998

Dear Mr Clegg,

I am told you are the new organsier of the annual Oxford and Cambridge boat race – congratulations! It's always a great spectacle and living in Barnes as we do we feel very much at the EPICENTER of the event.

It's nice to think that in this rapidly changing world of ours with all its nastiness and unpleasantness there are some things that do NOT change, and the boat race is one of them. The sight of those long, thin, craft snaking their way up the river, the flags, the bunting, the shouts of the crowd, the ever-present helicopter hovering overhead are the same today as when we first moved to Barnes in the sixties AND LONG MAY THEY LAST!

I am actually writing to you today in my capacity as an artist and 'portrait painter to the stars'. Watching the boat race this year it occurred to me how brilliant it would be to paint the oarsmen in 'oils' really CLOSE-UP, the grimaces, the sweat, the bared teeth, the taut muscles, the furrowed brows, the splashes from the oars etc. I'm sure you agree they would make stirring paintings. Then perhaps you could sponsor an exhibition?!

The only problem is the practical one of getting the artist (ME) close enough to the rowers during the actual race. I have given this some thought and come up with two possible solutions.

Firstly, I could obtain a small dinghy which would be attached by a short rope to one of the boats (Oxford or Cambridge – I'm not fussy) which could then tow me for the duration of the race. That would enable me to do a considerable amount of 'lightning' sketches which I could work from later in my studio.

Secondly, one of the teams could volunteer to take out an oarsman and I would simply take his place in the boat with my sketch pad and pencils, HEY PRESTO! I would then be able to rest my drawing board on the boat which would be handy.

From the sketches I would hope to paint about 20 pictures in oils which (with the sketches) would be enough for an exhibition.

Although it is several months until the next race I would appreciate it very much if you could let me know ASAP what you think of my proposal and if we can 'do business'.

I look forward to hearing from you and hopefully meeting you soon to discuss things further.

Yours sincerely,

Oscar Wendlow

OXFORD & CAMBRIDGE UNIVERSITY BOAT CLUBS

119 Albert Street
London NW1 7NB
Phone: 0171 267 3545
Fax: 0171 267 1355

Oscar Wendlow, Esq.,
'Portrait Painter to the Stars'.
  Cleveland Road,   28th October, 1998
Barnes,
London SW13 0AA   **PRIVATE AND CONFIDENTIAL**

Dear Mr. Wendlow,

Thank you for your letters of 24th September and 21st October (the latter included a five pound note which I return herewith with thanks). I did, indeed, receive your first letter but it arrived at the beginning of a fortnight's holiday and I had not had time to address is since my return.

Whilst the Clubs and the oarsmen will be very flattered by your excitement about the Race and your desire to capture this on canvas I am afraid that neither of your suggestions - being towed behind one of the eights or your sketching from within one of them - is practical, especially from the point of view of your safety. So I have, sadly, to decline with thanks.

In any event both Clubs are in straitened financial circumstances at present and could not undertake to sponsor an exhibition.

I really am very grateful for your interest and am sorry that my answer will disappoint you. Let me wish you well in your other endeavours.

Yours sincerely,

Duncan Clegg

Oscar Wendlow
'Portrait Painter To The Stars'
Cleveland Road, Barnes,
London SW13 0AA

Miss Philpott
M.O.D.
Room 8245,
Main Building,
Whitehall
London SW1A 2HB   26th October 1998

Dear Miss Philpott,

I have been given your name as the person who records UFO 'sightings'. I experienced a sighting in the early hours of Sunday morning and I would be very interested to hear what you 'make' of it.

I found it difficult to sleep on Saturday night and at about 12.15am went downstairs for a glass of milk. As you know it has been unseasonably mild of late and I decided to take my milk into the garden and sit on the bench. After a few moments I heard a 'distant roar' of engines getting louder and louder. Suddenly a huge 'craft' appeared over the house, heading in a westerly direction at speed. It was a large cigar shaped vehicle with big projectiles on each side like wings. It seemed to have two very bright lights at the front and a white light flashing round and round underneath. I think there were also coloured lights at the ends of the projectiles but I'm not certain - I WAS TOO BLOODY TERRIFIED! There also seemed to be a line of lights (which I took to be windows) along the side. It disappeared into the distance but as it did so it seemed to be getting closer to the ground.

As you can imagine I felt quite quite shaken. I thought of reporting it to the police immediately but decided to leave it until the following day. I then returned to bed and surprisingly fell asleep.

HOWEVER! in the morning my wife and I were having breakfast and listening to the radio when the presenter gave a time check. He said, 'Here is the news at nine o'clock.' I thought that seemed a bit early and looked at my watch which said TEN o'clock! Somehow, during the night I had gained A WHOLE HOUR! I said nothing to Joyce as I didn't want to scare her, but I am now beginning to wonder if I was ABDUCTED. I have checked my body for marks but found nothing. NEVERTHELESS I am very concerned. I have told NOBODY but you. I didn't sleep a wink last night and have made an appointment with my doctor to get some tranquillisers.

What do you think? Have I had a CLOSE ENCOUNTER?

Please write back as soon as possible.

Yours Sincerely,

Oscar Wendlow

PS   I am going to send this letter 'recorded' to make sure you get it.

From: Miss G F South, Secretariat(Air Staff)2a1a, Room 8245,
MINISTRY OF DEFENCE
Main Building, Whitehall, London SW1A 2HB

Telephone (Direct dial)
(Switchboard)
(Fax)

Mr O Wendlow
   Cleveland Road,
Barnes,
London.
SW13 0AA

Your reference

Our reference
D/Sec(AS/64/3
Date
28 October 1998

Dear Mr Wendlow,

Thank you for your letter of 26 October addressed to Miss Philpott regarding an 'unidentified flying object' which you saw above your home. This office is the focal point within the Ministry of Defence for correspondence of this nature. I have been asked to reply as Miss Philpott has now left this branch of the MOD.

First it may be useful if I explain that the Ministry of Defence examines any reports of 'unidentified flying objects' it receives solely to establish whether what was seen might have some defence significance; namely, whether there is any evidence that the United Kingdom's airspace might have been compromised by hostile or unauthorized foreign military activity.

Unless there is evidence of a potential threat to the United Kingdom from an external military source, and to date no 'UFO' report has revealed such evidence, we do not attempt to identify the precise nature of each sighting reported to us. We believe that rational explanations, such as aircraft lights or natural phenomena, could be found for them if resources were diverted for this purpose, but it is not the function of the MOD to provide this kind of aerial identification service. It would be an inappropriate use of defence resources if we were to do so. However, from your description of the craft, I believe you saw an airship.

As for your possible abduction theory, the clocks were put back one hour at 2am on Sunday and I think you will find that this would account for you gaining an hour. I hope this is helpful.

Yours sincerely,

Gaynor South.

89

Oscar Wendlow
'Portrait Painter To The Stars'
Cleveland Road, Barnes,
London SW13 0AA

Kilroy
Teddington Studios
Broom Road
Teddington TW11 9NT   26ᵗʰ October 1998

Dear 'Kilroy',

Well, well, well. So that's what daytime television is all about! Ha, ha! Last
Friday I spent the day at home (for reasons I won't go into) and after
breakfast was surprised to see my other 'alf switching on the telly. She
'confessed' that she is a BIG fan of yours and always tunes in to your show
when I am out working. I have never watched telly in the morning before so I
joined Joyce 'out of curiosity'.

Well, well, well! What an eye-opener! The title of the discussion was 'I DON'T
FANCY SHORT MEN' and it was COMPULSIVE viewing. You interviewed
the (short) radio DJ, 'Diddy' David Hamilton. Correct me if I'm wrong but
wasn't he wearing a 'syrup'? Perhaps you should have called the show 'I
don't fancy short men in wigs'! Ha, ha! Only joking. You also interviewed
several other 'vertically challenged' gents and their other 'alfs. I was shocked
at the way the women started talking about 'sex' and the differences between
tall and short men 'between the sheets'. I must be getting old! Ha, ha!

We thought it would be fun to take part in the show and wondered if you
could 'let us know' how to apply for tickets?

I have also thought about some possible topics for future discussions. 'I don't
fancy tall men'! or 'I don't fancy short women'! The list is endless!

Thank you for a thought - provoking and entertaining show. We look forward
to hearing from you.

Yours sincerely,

Oscar Wendlow

KILROY

Independent Image Film & TV Ltd
Teddington Studios
Broom Road
Teddington
Middlesex TW11 9NT
Tel: 0181 943 3555
Fax: 0181 943 3646
e-mail: info@kilroy.co.uk

Mr & Mrs O Wendlow
Cleveland Road
Barnes
London
SW13 OAA

28 October 1998

Dear Oscar,

Thank you for your letter. I always appreciate the opportunity to hear my viewers' opinions and ideas. As with all of the letters that I receive I will keep yours on file for future reference.

I hope that you will continue to watch and enjoy the show.

Yours sincerely,

Robert Kilroy-Silk

KILROY

Independent Image Film & TV Ltd is registered in England at 33-34 Soho Square, London W1V 6DP Registered No. 3621281

Brian Sewell (art critic)
C/o The Evening Standard
Northcliffe House,
2, Derry Street
London W8 5TS   22nd October 1998

Dear Mr Sewell,

I am currently arranging an exhibition of my portraits of 'celebrities' to be held next summer. The venue is yet to be confirmed but will hopefully be somewhere in the 'West end'. Obviously I would like as much 'publicity' for the show as possible, therefore a GOOD review would be helpful. However a BAD review would be unpleasant and 'negative'. I would very much like you to attend the opening and review my work but not if you are going to 'slag it off' so to speak.

My work is 'realistic', representational portraits of celebrities from the worlds of TV, film, politics, pop and the media and also of members of my family. They are realistic paintings of them in realistic settings. Nothing fancy, nothing quirky, nothing pretentious. Does that sound like the sort of thing you like?

If so, I would very much like you to come, if it was going to be 'favourable'. If you felt 'negative' about my work, however, I would prefer you to say nothing at all.

I am sure you understand, we artists are very sensitive people.

Having said all that, I'm sure you WILL like my work, I'M certainly very proud of it! Ha, ha!

Could you drop me a line and let me know what you think? I would be very grateful. I am enclosing a fiver to cover your expenses.

Yours sincerely,

Ocar Wendlow

PS   One thing I can say is, there certainly won't be any cows in formaldehyde in my show. Now that stuff really IS crap!

Evening Standard

2 Derry Street, London W8 5EE
Tel: 0171-938 6000

From **BRIAN SEWELL**

27 . x . 98 . Thanks for your letter.
Let me know if and when you have
your exhibition and I will then
make a point of seeing your work —
but I don't make studio visits —
no time for personal involvement.

Your £5 note amused me —
briefly — I return it with this
card — Sincerely [signature]

Oscar Wendlow
'Portrait Painter To The Stars'
Cleveland Road, Barnes,
London SW13 0AA

Brian Sewell
The Evening Standard
Northcliff Home
2 Derry Street
London W8 5EE   3rd November 1998

Dear Brian,

On Friday I received a postcard from you that was COMPLETELY
ILLEGIBLE. I only knew it was from you because it had your name printed on
it. I thought, 'That's ironic! A journalist who can't write' Ha, ha! Sorry, Brian, I
couldn't resist getting that in.

Seriously though, would you be so kind as to TYPE another letter so that I can
UNDERSTAND it? After all, we are in the 1990's, the age of computers! Quill
pens and bottles of ink went out yonks ago! Ha, ha!

Seriously though, I would very much like you to come to my exhibition next
summer and review it for the 'Evening Standard' if you think my work
sounds like your 'cup of tea'. Perhaps you could indicate in your reply
whether you think your review would be 'favourable' or 'unfavourable' so to
speak?!

You won't BELIEVE this, Brian! On Sunday I read about an artist in the
newspaper who makes sculptures out of COW DUNG! I thought, 'Brian
Sewell could go to that exhibition and write the shortest review in the world' -
'This work is a load of shit!' Ha, ha!

I look forward to hearing from you and hopefully meeting you next summer.
Cheers!

Yours Sincerely,

Ocar Wendlow

PS   I am enclosing a tenner to cover your expenses.

Evening Standard

From **BRIAN SEWELL**

2 Derry Street, London W8 5EE
Tel: 0171-938 6000

9 Nov 98. I'm sorry you cannot read my handwriting – I've no secretary to help with letters. The gist of the postcard was to tell you that what you suggest is impossible. The gist of this note is much the same.

B —

P.S. The Post Office obviously had no difficulty in reading the address —

Oscar Wendlow
'Portrait Painter To The Stars'
Cleveland Road, Barnes,
London SW13 0AA

Rt. Hon Tony Blair MP,
10 Downing Street
London SW1A 2AA   22nd October 1998

Dear Tony,

I won't beat about the bush. YOU HAVE GOT PROBLEM HAIR! How do I know? Because I have got problem hair too, or did have before it all fell out, Ha, ha! And it 'takes one to know one' as they say. It's that bit at the front! The back and sides can take care of themselves but that bit at the front doesn't know what the hell its doing! It's all over the place, and whatever you do to it, it goes off and does its own thing! It's got a mind of its own! It's like a wild animal that can't be tamed! AM I RIGHT?

Now, lets stop talking about the problem and talk about the SOLUTION! Next time Cherie roasts a chicken for your dinner save the leftover 'fat' and put it in the fridge. When it has solidified scrape off the white fat from the top and throw the brown jelly away (or save it for stock or put it in a sandwich, its very nice with mustard). Mix the white fat with swarfega, (the industrial hand cleaner for mechanics) two parts chicken fat to one part swarfega. It helps if you warm it up a little while mixing. Put it back in the fridge to 'firm up'. When it has 'firmed' remove it from the fridge and apply it to the hair generously and 'work' it in. Then comb it through and I guarantee your hair will do whatever you want. You CAN use the chicken fat on its own but the purpose of the swarfega is to disguise the smell of the fat. HEY PRESTO! PROBLEM SOLVED!

I don't know why I am telling you all this - I am a Tory! Never mind, let's just say I am being a good Samaritan.

Yours sincerely,

Ocar Wendlow

PS   My daughter, Anthea is a Labour supporter and has asked me to enclose £5 of her savings for your party funds.

PPS   Let me know how you get on. If you have any problems I can always send you some in the post ready made.

10 DOWNING STREET
LONDON SW1A 2AA

From the Political Office   20 November 1998

Dear Mr Wendlow,

Thank you for your letter of 22 October, together with your advice.

We were most grateful for the donation of £5.00 from your daughter, and have forwarded this to our fundraising department at Labour Party Headquarters, Millbank Tower, Millbank, London SW1P 4GT.

As you do not give your daughter's address, perhaps you would be kind enough to pass on our thanks for her generosity.

Yours sincerely,

Caroline Adams

CAROLINE ADAMS

Mr Oscar Wendlow

Mr Paul Burrell,
Princess Diana's Butler,
c/o Kensington Palace
London W8 4PU

Dear Mr Burrell,

My other 'alf and I are 'true blue Tory royalists' and we would like to give you a word of advice. CALM DOWN! Every time we open a newspaper or magazine there you are at some party grinning like a 'Cheshire cat'! Before Diana died we had never heard of you, NOW YOU'RE EVERYWHERE! To be honest, it doesn't look good and people are 'beginning to talk.'

We think you would be well advised to step out of the limelight and keep a low profile (after all you're only a butler, not some star) and if you must attend some party or function, at least try and LOOK SAD!

Yours sincerely

Ocar Wendlow

P.S. £10 enclosed for Diana's charity fund.

Princess of Wales Memorial Fund

The County Hall, Westminster Bridge Road, London SE1 7PB
Tel: 0171-902 5500 Fax: 0171-902 5511

6 November 1998

Oscar Wendlow Esq
 Cleveland Road
Barnes
LONDON SW13 0AA

Dear Mr Wendlow

I am writing on behalf of everyone involved with the Diana, Princess of Wales Memorial Fund to thank you very much indeed for your donation of £10.00.

There has been enormous support of the Memorial Fund by so many people and we are simply overwhelmed by the generosity and numbers of those who are contributing, from all walks of life, both at home and abroad. It is a wonderful tribute to the life and work of the Princess.

Please accept our sincerest thanks.

Yours sincerely

JACQUELINE ALLEN

Oscar Wendlow
'Portrait Painter To The Stars'
Cleveland Road, Barnes,
London SW13 0AA

Leslie Waddington
Waddingtons
11 Cork Street
London W1X 2LT   22nd October 1998

Dear Mr Waddington

I wrote to you in October of last year asking if you would be interested in 'staging' an exhibition of my portraits of 'celebrities' and members of my family. Somebody called Hester van Roiyen replied 'in the negative'.

However, I am now writing again in the hope that you might 'reconsider' your decision in the light of recent developments.

FIRSTLY, Maggie Kouni, the editor of Hello! Magazine is very keen to cover the 'private view' of any exhibition of mine!

SECONDLY, Peter Stringfellow is a personal friend and I have asked him to supply a dozen or so gorgeous girls from Cabaret of Angels to attend the opening!

THIRDLY, I am currently lining up celebrity chef 'Marco Pierre White' to supply snacks and nibbles on the night!

FOURTHLY, I have been in touch with Lt. Col. Sean O'Dwyer, HRH prince Edward's private secretary and am hoping to get the Prince and Miss Sophie Rhys Jones to 'appear' at the opening!

FIFTHLY, I have just heard from the Nominations Unit at the Cabinet office that I have an honour 'in the pipeline'!

SIXTHLY, I am just about to be made a member of the Chelsea Arts Club and the Garrick!

SEVENTHLY, I have approached Brian Sewell, the art critic of the Evening Standard about doing a 'positive' review of my work!

Impressive stuff, I am sure you will agree. Therefore I hope that you might think again before turning me down this time. I look forward to hearing from you with a more positive attitude.

Yours sincerely,

Oscar Wardlow

£5 enclosed to cover your costs.

Waddington Galleries

11 CORK STREET LONDON W1X 2LT
TEL: 0171 437 8611 / 439 6262 FAX: 0171 734 4146

Recorded Delivery

LW/SEC

31 October 1998

Mr Oscar Wendlow
'Portrait Painter to the Stars'
  Cleveland Road
Barnes
London
SW13 OAA

Dear Mr Wendlow

Thank you for your recent letter.

I am afraid that I would not be interested in staging an exhibition of your portraits of celebrities and of members of your family as this falls completely outside the policy of the gallery.

Meanwhile, thank you for sending the £5 to cover our costs which I duly return to you.

Yours sincerely

LESLIE WADDINGTON

Enc:

(also 12 & 34 Cork Street) Directors: L.Waddington, A.Bernstein, Sir Thomas Lighton Bt, Lord McAlpine of West Green, H.van Roijen, S.F.Saunders Registered Number 872520 England. Registered Office: Waddington Galleries Ltd 11 Cork Street London W1X 2LT

Oscar Wendlow
'Portrait Painter To The Stars'
Cleveland Road, Barnes,
London SW13 0AA

HRH Queen Elizabeth
Buckingham Palace
London SW1A 1AA   4th December 1998

Dear Ma'am,

I was sorry to read about the death of 'Poet Laureate', Ted Hughes the other week What a shame, and he wasn't very old! I must admit I am not familiar with his work but I know he was 'highly regarded'.

It occurred to me that his 'demise' must leave a vacancy for a new poet Laureate and I wondered if I could 'throw my hat into the ring'. I would be very interested in the job and honoured if you would consider me for it. I am a cab driver by profession but I am very artistic hence the title 'Portrait Painter to the Stars'. As well as painting I am interested in anything 'cultural'; plays, songs, opera, poetry, classical music, films with subtitles, radio 4 etc. I haven't written much in the way of poetry but if you gave me the post I promise I would 'knuckle down' and churn them out. It's easier than painting.

Here is a sample I wrote last night:-
DON'T LET THE SUN GO DOWN ON A QUARREL
Your hair flickered in the light from the telly
Then you turned and stared
I turned my head towards yours and
Sensed something in the air
Then your thoughts metamorphosed into words
And I was taken by surprise
Cross words metamorphosed into crosser words
And I was even more surprised
You said this and you said that
And you said the other
I was surprised at the things you said
And your harsh words made me judder
'Hang on a minute'
'I'm not taking this lying down'
So I stood up to take the dog for a walk
Until you had calmed down
When I returned she was calmer and
I made her a cup of tea
I sat beside her and she said sorry
We kissed and made up and switched on
The news which showed the Queen at Balmoral
One thing that I always will say is
'Don't let the sun go down on a quarrel'.

I hope you like it. There are plenty more where that came from. Please let me know if you would like to see some more and if I stand a good chance of getting the job? Many thanks. The more I do the better they will get.

Yours sincerely,

Oscar Wendlow

BUCKINGHAM PALACE

10th December, 1998

Dear Mr. Wendlow,

I am commanded by The Queen to write and thank you for your letter about the post of Poet Laureate, and for the poem you included with it.

Her Majesty thought it was kind of you to suggest that, as a result of the sad death of Ted Hughes, you yourself might be a suitable candidate for this post. Since it is the responsibility of the Prime Minister to produce a list of possible successors for The Queen's approval, may I suggest that you approach No. 10 Downing Street direct? I should warn you, however, that it is probably that there are already a number of candidates being considered.

Yours sincerely,

Katryn Dydale.

Lady-in-Waiting

O. Wendlow, Esq.

1O DOWNING STREET
LONDON SW1A 2AA

From the Office of the Secretary for Appointments
(J. H. Holroyd, C.B)

27 January 1999

Dear Mr Wendlow

Thank you for your letter of 19th January about the succession to the late Ted Hughes as Poet Laureate.

The Prime Minister has asked me to carry out a full consultation about possible successors with organisations and individuals who are knowledgeable about modern poetry and poets. During that process I shall certainly take account of your commendation.

Yours sincerely

Alison Roberts

PP

JOHN HOLROYD

Oscar Wendlow Esq

Oscar Wendlow
'Portrait Painter To The Stars'
Cleveland Road, Barnes,
London SW13 0AA

J. H. Holroyd C. B.
10, Downing Street
London
SW1A 2AA

4th February 1999

Dear John Holroyd,

I am CHUFFED TO BITS to hear you are considering my application for the post of 'Poet Laureate'. I am enclosing £20 for you personally as a small token of my gratitude. As I said in my previous letter, I have not 'done a lot' in the way of poetry but if you give me the job all that will change and I will CHURN THEM OUT. Here's one I wrote last night :

FOOTBALL IS EXCITING

Football is exciting,
Oh yes it is.
Football is thrilling,
Oh yes it is.
Football is great,
Oh yes it is.
Oh yes, oh yes.
I'm not exaggerating,
Football is definitely exciting.

(copyright) Oscar Wendlow 1999

I wrote that in FIVE MINUTES would you believe?! Let me know if you want to see some more!
Can you also let me know WHEN you will make your final decision and if there is ANYTHING I can do to increase my chances??!! I AM VERY KEEN TO GET THIS JOB! I have been a taxi driver for 23 years and am SICK TO DEATH of it. It's so UNCREATIVE!

Also, could you let me know how much I would get paid and are there any 'perks' with the job (company car, health insurance, pension scheme etc.)

I look forward to hearing from you and please remember I am VERY KEEN!

Yours sincerely,

Oscar Wendlow

1O DOWNING STREET
LONDON SW1A 2AA

From the Secretary for Appointments
J. H. Holroyd, C.B.

9 February 1999

Dear Mr Wendlow,

Thank you for your letter of 4th February.

I am afraid that I could not accept any money from you, however kindly meant. Accordingly I'm returning your £20.

The consultation on the next Poet Laureate is continuing with names of some very eminent nationally known poets being considered. As to your own chances, I am afraid that I can say no more than I did in my letter of 27th January. It is not yet clear when the name of the new Poet Laureate will be announced.

Yours sincerely,

John Holroyd

JOHN HOLROYD

Oscar Wendlow Esq

Oscar Wendlow
'Portrait Painter To The Stars'
Cleveland Road, Barnes,
London SW13 0AA

Mohammed Al Fayed
Fulham Football Club
Fulham
London SW6 6HH   2nd March 1999

Dear Mohammed Al Fayed,

I am writing to you about a rather delicate matter. My father-in-law (who is a huge Fulham fan) lives at the end of Finlay Street adjacent to Fulham Football Ground. He has been very ill over the last three years with heart problems and on the 28th of March goes into Charing Cross Hospital for a triple by-pass. He is 78 and very weak so we do not know if he will survive the operation. If he does then he will need a very long, slow period of recuperation. The consultant has told us that he will require 24 hour supervision and complete peace and quiet for at least the first five weeks. This is why I am writing to you. Albert's house is so close to the football ground that the noise of the crowd during 'home' games is quite deafening. Being a Fulham fan Albert always gets worked up and over-excited by the noise. This is what concerns us. If he was to get 'hyped-up' during his recovery period the results could be dangerous and even fatal. I have discussed this with our GP who agrees it is a serious problem, however his only suggestion was 'ear-plugs'. I fear this would not be adequate to block out the roar of the crowd when a goal is scored or when the singing is at its peak. I am therefore writing to ask if you could very kindly help us out with this difficult situation.

Would you be prepared to make an announcement over the tannoy system at the 'home' games explaining about Albert's condition and asking the supporters to sing and cheer as quietly as possible? It also occurs to me that you could use the score board to remind fans during the match with simple messages; SSSSHH! NO SHOUTING PLEASE! PLEASE SING QUIETLY! ETC. ETC. It would mean an awful lot to us if you could consider this. Obviously we are doing everything in our powers to aid Albert's recovery but it would be great if you could help too. He is a lifelong Fulham supporter and it would be tragic if he was to be killed by the shouts of his fellow fans. I look forward to hearing from you.

Yours sincerely,

Ocar Wendlow

RECORDED DELIVERY

I am enclosing £5 to cover your expenses.

Fulham Football Club

Craven Cottage, Stevenage Road, London SW6 6HH
Tel: 0171 893 8383 Fax: 0171 384 4715 Website: www.fulhamfc.co.uk

Established 1879

Our Ref NR/EG/7

Oscar Wendlow
  Cleveland Road
BARNES
London
SW13 0AA

17th March 1999

Dear Mr Wendlow,

Thank you for your letter, regarding your Father-in-law's delicate condition, which the Chairman, Mr Al Fayed has asked me to respond to on his behalf.

I'm very sorry to hear of your Father-in-law's ill health and I hope he makes a full recovery from his operation.

A fundamental part of being a football fan is being able to support your team and yes this involves cheering and shouting, especially when a goal is scored. I do sympathise with your problem but we feel it would be impossible to ask our supporters to kerb their passion for the team.

Unfortunately we do not have a "score board" as such so our main channel of communication with fans at a match is over our tannoy system, this system is louder than all the fans put together so putting a message over the tannoy would only add to your inconvenience.

I do sympathise with your problem and the local residence are of paramount importance to Fulham Football Club but I'm afraid what you are asking is an impossible task which we are not in a position to fulfil.

On the up side we only have 5 home matches left after the date of the operation, which are as follows:

Saturday 10th April   Fulham V Wigan

Tuesday 13th April   Fulham V Gillingham

Fulham Football Club (1987) Limited. Registered in England No 2114486 VAT Reg No. 696 9485 49

official club sponsor   official club line   official kit supplier

108

Fulham Football Club

Craven Cottage, Stevenage Road, London SW6 6HH
Tel: 0171 893 8383 Fax: 0171 384 4715 Website: www.fulhamfc.co.uk

Established 1879

Wednesday 21st April Fulham V Millwall

Saturday 24th April   Fulham V Wrexham

Saturday 8th May   Fulham V Preston

I hope this helps you to plan alternative arrangements for your Father-in Law.

I have enclosed your £5 as no costs have been incurred.

If I can be of further assistance in this matter please do not hesitate to contact me.

Yours sincerely

Neil Rodford
Managing Director

Enc

Fulham Football Club (1987) Limited. Registered in England No 2114486 VAT Reg No. 696 9485 49

official club sponsor   official club line   official kit supplier

Alexandra Shulman,
Vogue,
Vogue House,
Hanover Square,
London W1R 0AD

2nd October 1998

Dear Alexandra Shulman

Last night I found my daughter Anthea crying in her bedroom. When I asked her what was wrong she said, 'I'm so ugly, Dad.' I sat down on her bed, put my arm around her and said, 'But, you've got a beautiful personality, love!' She continued sobbing, then I noticed a copy of Vogue behind her. She buys it every month and it ALWAYS makes her unhappy. She looks at the pictures of all the beautiful models, then looks at herself in the mirror and understandably bursts into tears. It may seem a heartless thing for a father to say about his own daughter but she **is** ugly. There is no denying it. She gets it from her mother's side. My mother-in-law looks like a cross between Les Dawson and Tommy Cooper with a dash of Robin Cook.

We took Anthea to a plastic surgeon (at her insistence) but he threw his hands up and said he couldn't make a 'silk purse out of a pigs ear.'

Nevertheless, life would be a lot more bearable for 'plain Janes' if they were not constantly bombarded by images of beautiful women in the media. I wonder if A. you are aware of the unhappiness your magazine causes and B. if you would consider using some 'plain' models to balance things up a bit?

I look forward to hearing from you.

Yours sincerely

Oscar Wendlow

The Condé Nast Publications Ltd.
Vogue House, Hanover Square, London, WIR 0AD
Fax: editorial 0171 408 0559 advertising 0171 460 6354
Tel: 0171 499 9080

23 October 1998

Oscar Wendlow
  Cleveland Road
Barnes
SW13 0AA

Dear Oscar Wendlow

I apologise for taking such a long time to reply to your letter.

I do appreciate that it's an endless problem for teenagers to relate their own appearance to that of the models in the magazine, but I'm afraid that fashion magazines will always need to feature beautiful women.

I very much hope your daughter does not continue to feel unhappy by the magazine which also features a wide range of women who are stars in various fields of life.

With best wishes

ALEXANDRA SHULMAN
Editor

Registered office as above. Registered in London no. 226900

Oscar Wendlow
'Portrait Painter To The Stars'
Cleveland Road, Barnes,
London SW13 0AA

Jenny Tongue MP
House of Commons
London SW1A 0AA   4th December 1998

Dear Jenny Tongue,

I am writing to you as our MP to say that I am FED UP with dogs fouling the
footpaths in this area. It is disgusting and unhygienic and something HAS TO BE
DONE!

My other 'alf, Joyce has become a keen runner of late and is currently in training for
the Venice marathon. This involves a lot of 'roadwork' after dark which has become
extremely hazardous. She has slipped over on faeces twice this year and this evening
she returned home yet again with it all over one of her brand new Nike's.

If we can have parking attendants policing car parking why can't we have dog faeces
attendants policing dogs and their owners?

I suggest 'Faeces Returning Officers' (F.R.O.'s for short) who would follow dog-
walkers at a distance. If the dog fouled the pavement and the owner failed to pick it
up the F.R.O. would do so, then follow the dog walker home. When he or she had
gone indoors the officer would drop the faeces through the letterbox or smear it all
over the front door.

Do you think London Borough of Richmond Upon Thames would be prepared to
sponsor such a scheme? Please let me know. SOMETHING HAS TO BE DONE! I
look forward to hearing from you.

Yours sincerely,

Oscar Wendlow

DR JENNY TONGE MP

HOUSE OF COMMONS
LONDON SW1A 0AA

December 9 1998

Mr Oscar Wendlow
Cleveland Road
Barnes
London SW13 0AA

Dear Mr Wendlow,

Thank you for your letter of December 4.

I agree with you that the fouling of footpaths by dogs is disgusting and
unhygienic but I am not certain that your idea is totally practical - certainly not
the direct action you suggest!

Local Councils are able to prosecute people who allow their dogs to foul
footpaths but for legal measures to be successful, the dogs must actually be
'caught' in the act. The costs of having your F.R.O.'s on every street would, I
respectfully suggest, be prohibitive.

On a more encouraging note I am delighted by the awareness there is on this
issue by young people in our local schools. Almost every time I visit a school I
am asked by Kids what can be done. They are doing an excellent job in
spreading the message and making real changes.

There is hope!

Yours sincerely,

pp : **Jenny Tonge (Dr.)**
Member of Parliament
for Richmond Park

Oscar Wendlow
'Portrait Painter To The Stars'
Cleveland Road, Barnes,
London SW13 0AA

Melvyn Bragg
The South Bank Show
LWT
The London TV Centre
Upper Ground
London SE1 9LT   4th December 1998

Dear Mr Bragg

I watched the South Bank Show last night which featured the Playwrite, Harold
Pinter. I must say that I was shocked at the bad language he used. You'd think an
educated bloke like that would know better. I was even more shocked that you just sat
there nodding and made no attempt to shut him up! Is it not part of your job
description to keep things 'under control'? Could you not have asked him to desist?
Or at least put in some bleeps! One of his poems contained several 'fucks' and a
smattering of 'shits'. Did you HAVE to select THAT poem for the programme? Could
you not have a chosen a CLEANER (and perhaps more cheerful) one? I notice your
show is now on later then ever and hope you are not resorting to the use of SHOCK
TACTICS to attract viewers. You're above that, Melvyn!

If the name looks familiar it is because I wrote to you about a year ago asking if you
would like me to paint your portrait. You sent me a very courteous reply (which I have
kept) explaining that you were too busy.

I am now writing to ask if you would be interested in doing a South Bank Show on
ME? Admittedly I am not famous (yet, Ha, ha) but I AM a 'bit of a character' and I'm
sure your viewers would find me 'entertaining'.

I am a London Taxi driver by trade and have a 'veritable plethora' of amusing
anecdotes to tell. I have picked up several 'stars' over the years including the great Sir
Lawrence Olivier (before he died) and Carol Barnes, the newscaster. I also paint
portraits of celebrities from the 'arts and media' and am currently trying to organise an
exhibition of them at a top 'west end' gallery.

For the programme I imagine you interviewing me sitting in the back of my cab (with
a cameraman) while I take you for a (free) ride around London. I would show you the
landmarks of my life, birthplace (Deptford), schools etc. and tell you my life story
'intercut' with shots of my paintings.

I think it could be a very interesting programme and (to be honest) a lot more
interesting than Mr Pinter (let's face it, Melvyn, he didn't exactly have much 'bounce
to the ounce') People would be much more interested in paintings of celebrities. I
hope you agree and very much look forward to hearing from you.

Yours in anticipation,

Oscar Wendlow

THE SOUTH BANK SHOW

EDITED AND PRESENTED BY

MELVYN BRAGG

12th January 1999

Oscar Wendlow
  Cleveland Road
Barnes
London
SW13 OAA

Dear Oscar Wendlow

Many thanks for your letter. Your first letter must have gone astray as we try to be very conscientious here.

I don't think that we can manage a South Bank Show about your work. We do, however, have a good deal of 'bounce the ounce'. I suggest you get in touch with Jim Allen, Controller of Factual Programmes.

Good luck and best wishes,

Yours sincerely

MELVYN BRAGG

London Weekend Television. The London Television Centre, Upper Ground, London SE1 9LT. Telephone: 0171 620 1620 Fax: 0171 261 3782
Registered in England (No. 2446504) Registered Office: The London Television Centre, Upper Ground, London SE1 9LT

Oscar Wendlow
'Portrait Painter To The Stars'
Cleveland Road, Barnes,
London SW13 0AA

David Attenborough
The Life of Birds
C/O BBC Natural History Unit
Whiteladies Road
Bristol BS8 2LR   4th December 1998

Dear David Attenborough

Thankyou for your SUPERB series on the life of birds, I have never seen
such brilliant wildlife photography before. It is spectacular stuff and to be
honest, my other 'alf and I have been GOBSMACKED at the brutality and
violence that takes place in the animal kingdom.

I was wondering if you have ever thought of doing a series on domestic
pets? The reason I ask you this is that I find a lot of our dogs behaviour
quite odd and highly entertaining. It would be interesting to see a series
which tried to explain the behaviours of our common domestic pets.

For example; Why does our Springer Spaniel, Plod, always continue to bark
for eight minutes after the postman has been? Why does he howl at the
television when we watch Catchphrase but sit still and quiet through Noels
House Party? And why does he sit on the floor, raise his back paws up a
couple of inches then walk his front legs forwards, dragging his bottom
across the carpet? Is this some kind of ancient mating ritual?

As we are a nation of dog and cat lovers I am sure a series of this nature
would prove very popular. You would be very welcome to come and film
Plod's 'antics' at any time, in fact I think he could be something of a star!
He certainly keeps us entertained.

I look forward to hearing your thoughts and thankyou again for a
fascinating series.

Yours sincerely,

Oscar Wendlow

from Sir David Attenborough CH, FRS

10·12·98

Dear Mr Wendlow,

Thank you for your letter.
The BBC has, in the past, produced
programmes about the behaviour of
domestic pets; but I dare say
it is time they produced some
more.

I fear, however, it cannot
be me who does so as my filming
schedules are full for the next
three years.

Thank you none the less
for the suggestion.

With best wishes

David Attenborough

Oscar Wendlow
'Portrait Painter To The Stars'
Cleveland Road, Barnes,
London SW13 0AA

Charles Saumarez Smith
The National Portrait Gallery,
2 St. Martins Place,
London WC2H 0HE   19th January 1999

Dear Charles Saumarez Smith,

I was surprised to read over the weekend that you are currently holding an exhibition of CARTOONS by Gerald Scarfe, the cartoonist who is married to the 'toothsome' Jane Asher who used to go out with poor old ex-Beatle Paul McCartney (wasn't it sad about Linda!)

It seems strange that a respected institution like our National Portrait Gallery in Trafalgar Square should be exhibiting the work of a mere CARTOONIST! The word 'downmarket' comes to mind.

Don't get me wrong! I've nothing against cartoonists. On the contrary, I am a big fan of Fred by Rupert Fawcett which appears in the Mail on Sunday each week. I just think they should stay in newspapers where they belong and not try to 'worm' their way upmarket into the serious art world.

You are our National Portrait Gallery! Surely you should be exhibiting serious portraits, not JOKES! If you are short on serious painters I would like to nominate MYSELF. I have been painting portraits of celebrities from the 'arts and media' for some three years now and have a collection of over eighty. Would you be interested in holding an exhibition of my work? The pictures are all oils on board and measure approx. 3ft by 2ft. I have enclosed some photos of a few (which do not do them justice).

I would be happy to sell them - I was thinking of £300 each. What do you think? I would also be willing to donate some to your permanent exhibition.

I hope you are interested and very much look forward to hearing from you.

Yours sincerely,

Oscar Wendlow

PS   PLEASE RETURN THE PHOTOS! (They cost a fortune these days!)

NATIONAL PORTRAIT GALLERY

From
THE DIRECTOR
CHARLES SAUMAREZ SMITH PHD

25 January 1999

Oscar Wendlow
  Cleveland Road
Barnes
LONDON
SW13 0AA

Dear Mr Wendlow

Thank you very much for your letter of 19 January 1999 concerning the fact that we have exhibited the cartoons by Gerald Scarfe. I hope that you will by now have had an opportunity of seeing the exhibition, which has been extremely successful.

As to your own work, I very much regret that I do not feel that we could submit it to the Board of Trustees; however I am grateful to you for bringing it to our attention.

Yours sincerely

Charles Saumarez Smith PhD
Director

Oscar Wendlow
'Portrait Painter To The Stars'
Cleveland Road, Barnes,
London SW13 0AA

Michael Ancram
Conservative Party Central Office
32 Smith Square
London SW1P 3HH   19th January 1999

Dear Mr Ancram,

I am a lifelong supporter of the Conservative Party and have made considerable contributions to your funds over the years. As such I feel entitled to give my opinions and advice from time to time and this is ONE SUCH OCCASION. Lets face it, things are not going well for us at the moment (despite Labours own-goals) and William Hague's sacking of Lord Cranborne marked our lowest point to date. To be HONEST I am NOT the biggest William Hague fan on the planet. HOWEVER, he is our leader and as such should get BEHIND him, SUPPORT him, HELP him in any ways we can and start 'singing from the same hymn sheet'!

IMAGE is all important these days. Look at Blair! He was elected because of his carefully crafted image which portrayed him as young, fresh-faced, 'hip', dynamic, guitar playing, etc. In a word - YOUTHFUL! He made poor old John Major look out-of-date and washed up'. What worries me is that Blair is making William Hague look old and out of date too! THEREFORE, some action needs to be taken to rescue the situation. I suggest you get some 'image-makers' in to 're-vamp' our leader and give him a more 'youthful' look. The first and most obvious thing to do is COVER UP THAT BALD HEAD! I happen to have a friend, Leo, who owns 'Short and Curlies' hair salon in Shepherds Bush which specialises in wig-making. I am sure he would be happy to give Mr Hague a free consultation - Let me know!

I also suggest he keeps the lovely Ffion at his side at all times! She is definitely his trump card. Could she sit beside him in the House of Commons?

Also, I think Bill Hague sounds a lot more punchy than William! How about it? Let me know what you think.

I shall be sending you another contribution to funds shortly and look forward to hearing from you in the meantime. Keep up the good work, you seem to be doing a good job!

I WANT TO SEE THE TORIES BACK IN POWER! LET'S GET TO WORK!

Yours sincerely,

Oscar Wendlow

CONSERVATIVE

Oscar Wendlow Esq
 Cleveland Road
Barnes
London SW13 OAA

22 January 1999

Dear Mr Wendlow

The Party Chairman has asked me to thank you for your letter of 19 January and to reply on his behalf.

Mr Ancram is grateful for your support for the Party and has carefully noted your comments. Mr Ancram shares Mr Hague's determination to hold the Government to account and provide an alternative to them.

The coming year will be very important for the Conservative Party. Even though there are no local elections in London, across the country we have the opportunity not just to win hundreds of council seats but also to win back control of councils too. In Europe we have a real chance of increasing our representation in the European Parliament and helping to turn back the tide of Euro-socialism. In Scotland and Wales we have the opportunity to put the Conservatives back on the electoral map as the only Party committed to low taxes, good services and the Union.

1999 will also be the year in which the Conservative Party begins to develop a fresh, positive and compassionate agenda for the next century. Mr Ancram very much hopes that all Party members will take the opportunities that the reforms to the Party have given them to play a full part in this thorough overall of our policies.

Thank you again for writing.

Yours sincerely,

Ian Philps
Chairman's Correspondence Officer

The Conservative Party
32 Smith Square, Westminster,
London SW1P 3HH
Tel: 0171 222 9000 Fax: 0171 222 1135
www.conservative-party.org.uk

Oscar Wendlow
'Portrait Painter To The Stars'
Cleveland Road, Barnes,
London SW13 0AA

Richard Branson,
Virgin Airship & Balloon,
Unit 1
Stafford Park 12
Telford
TF3 3BJ

21st January 1999

Dear Richard Branson,

YOU ARE A HERO! I mean it! I've followed your career with great interest over the years and it is STAGGERING what you have achieved! I sometimes wish you'd slow down and give the rest of us a chance. Ha, ha!

I well remember your first Virgin record shop in Notting Hill Gate in the early seventies. You had big cushions on the floor and headphones attached to the walls so that the punters could lie around and listen to the 'far out sounds man', ha, ha! You've certainly come a long way since then. WELL DONE! And why haven't you received an honour yet? It's a mystery to me! You should have been LORD Branson yonks ago!

I was so sorry you didn't manage to complete your hot air balloon trip round the world BUT I am delighted to hear you are going to have another BASH. That is why I am writing to you.

Would you consider taking along an 'artist in residence' on your next trip, to record the adventure in oils? Namely ME! Ha, ha! I usually paint portraits of celebrities and stars but its a bit limiting (YAWN Ha, ha!) and nothing would give me greater pleasure than painting a real-life ADVENTURE! I bet you get some knock-out views up there, mountain ranges, snow-capped 'peaks' etc. BRILLIANT STUFF! I would also want to paint and sketch the drama INSIDE the capsule, the tense expressions, the furrowed brows and beads of perspiration, the glowing lights on the instrument panel etc. AND the INFORMAL moments too; you cooking breakfast or lying on your bunk reading a magazine or larking about with Pers Lindstraum and the other bloke. (I know you have a great sense of fun!)

Then when we returned I could have an exhibition and invite all the press. The paintings might even make a book! Then we could give a percentage of sales to charity! What do you think? Please let me know as soon as possible and keep up the good work, Richard. You are an inspiration to us all.

Yours sincerely,

Ocar Wendlow

PS   Just out of interest, how do you go to the toilet in the capsule?
PPS   I would also be happy to 'muck in' if there was a drama on board.

1 STAFFORD PARK 12
TELFORD SHROPSHIRE
TF3 3BJ

TEL: 01952 292945
FAX: 01952 292930

22nd January 1999

Oscar Wendlow Esq
Portrait Painter to the Stars
  Cleveland Road
Barnes
LONDON
SW13 OAA

Dear Oscar

Your letter addressed to Richard, has been forwarded to me for reply, as Project Director on the recent global attempt.

While the idea is very appealing I am afraid we do not have room for an extra person in the capsule.

I am sorry to disappoint you, but thank you for taking the time to write in with your idea.

Yours sincerely

MICHAEL KENDRICK

VIRGIN AIRSHIP AND BALLOON COMPANY LIMITED REGISTERED NO. 2132831 ENGLAND VAT REGISTERED NO. 539 1054 51
REGISTERED OFFICE 120 CAMPDEN HILL ROAD LONDON W8 7AR

Oscar Wendlow
'Portrait Painter To The Stars'
Cleveland Road, Barnes.
London SW13 0AA

Jeremy Paxman
Newsnight
BBC TV Centre
Wood Lane
W12 7RJ   19th January 1999

Dear Jeremy Paxman,

You have come in for a lot of criticism for your interviewing technique over the years but I AM ALL FOR IT! If people like you didn't give our politicians a good 'grilling' WHO WOULD? They'd get away with MURDER.

People call you 'smug'. Well, so WHAT? You're successful, you're famous, you're rich, you're good at your job. You DESERVE to be smug! Hells bells! If YOU can't be smug, who can? Good luck to you, Jeremy! Incidentally, do you call yourself Jeremy or Paxo or is that merely a press term?

I was particularly impressed with your interrogation of William Hague a few weeks ago, over the Lord Cranborne sacking (what a fiasco!) I happen to be a lifelong 'true blue' Tory but I am not at all happy with our current 'leader'. I don't think he has got 'what it takes' and lacks 'charisma'. What do you think? For years I regarded Maggie Thatcher's reign as 'the good old days' but now I am looking back on John Major in the same way! Heaven forbid I ever find myself talking about William Hague as 'the good old days'! If so, I might as well put a gun to my head, ha, ha! Only joking!

As you can see from my heading 'Portrait Painter to the Stars' I am an artist (Sundays only, ha, ha!) who specialises in paintings of celebrities and people in 'public life' whom I admire. I wondered if you might be interested in 'sitting' for a portrait. I would need about half a dozen sittings of three hours duration for a decent-sized portrait in oils. If I was pleased with the picture it could then go into my forthcoming exhibition this summer and I would give you first option on purchasing it.

I try to make my paintings as flattering as possible and offer all sitters 'blemish enhancement', i.e. if there is a particular feature about themselves they dislike like a double a chin for example, I can reduce it in the painting. Forgive me for being personal but you do have a fairly 'prominent' nose. I would happy to reduce it's size if you wanted. It's entirely up to you.

What I need to know now is, are you interested and available for sittings day or evening? I very much look forward to hearing from you and keep up the good work!

Yours sincerely,

Oscar Wendlow

British Broadcasting Corporation Room Television Centre Wood Lane London W12 7RJ Telephone 0181 624 9800
Fax 0181 743 1102 E-mail newsnight@bbc.co.uk

Newsnight

26 January 1999

Oscar Wendlow
'Portrait Painter to the Stars'
  Cleveland Road
Barnes
SW13 0AA

Dear Oscar Wendlow,

Many thanks for your invitation to sit for a portrait. While it's highly flattering to be invited, I'm afraid I don't think I can find the time.

Yours sincerely,

Jeremy Paxman

1

Oscar Wendlow
'Portrait Painter To The Stars'
Cleveland Road, Barnes,
London SW13 0AA

Nicholas Witchel (newscaster)   27th January 1999
Nine O'clock News
BBC TV Centre
Wood Lane
London W12 7RJ

Dear Nicholas Witchel,

I am a portrait painter who specialises in paintings of TV celebrities and personalities. I have recently had an idea for a project which I hope may interest you. It will be an entire exhibition of paintings of people with red hair, to be called, 'REDHEADS AT THE REAR END OF THE MILLENNIUM'.

Other 'redheads' I am approaching include Paddy Ashdown, Ann Robinson, The Duchess of York, Neil Kinnock, Mick Hucknall (of Simply Red) and Chris Evans. I would require you to attend at least 6 three -hour sittings at my home and attend a 'group' photoshoot where I would gather all the 'redheads' together for a unique and historic photograph. I also hope you would have no objections to being interviewed about your 'experiences' as a 'redhead'. I plan to turn the paintings, interviews and photos into a limited edition coffee table book (Hodder Headline are very keen). If everyone is prepared to give their services free of charge then I would donate 10% of the proceeds to charity (retired taxi drivers fund).

I do hope you will be interested in taking part in this unique project which I am hoping will put redheads firmly 'on the map'!

I look forward to hearing from you.

Yours sincerely

Ocar Wendlow

P.S. I will be happy to cover your expenses.

BBC News

1 February 1999.

Oscar Wendlow,
 Cleveland Road,
London SW13 0AA.

Dear Mr Wendlow,

Thanks for your letter: what an unusual project!

I've no objection in principle to taking part, though I would be interested to learn a little more (who, for example, is definitely taking part?) before taking a final decision.

The other thing that would concern me is the prospect of attending "at least 6 three hour sittings". That seems rather an excessive amount of sitting.

Why don't you contact me again when the details have firmed up and I would be delighted to discuss it further. My number here at the BBC is 0181 624

Yours sincerely,

NICHOLAS WITCHELL.

1

127

Oscar Wendlow
'Portrait Painter To The Stars'
Cleveland Road, Barnes,
London SW13 0AA

Nicholas Witchell (newscaster)
Nine O'clock News
BBC TV Centre
Wood Lane
London W12 7RJ   4th February 1999

Dear Nick,

Thank you for your letter of 1st February 1999. I am CHUFFED TO BITS that you are interested in 'coming on board' in this exciting project.

I am happy to confirm Chris Evans, Mick Hucknall, Geri Halliwell and Neil Kinnock (although he may only be available for one 'sitting'). The Duchess of York is interested but like you her office has requested more details. Sadly, Paddy Ashdown has declined due to being 'over-committed' but he gave 'REDHEADS AT THE REAR END OF THE MILLENNIUM' his full support and wished us well. I have yet to hear from Anne Robinson (perhaps you could give her a nudge). Would you like to suggest any other 'celebrity' redheads who might be interested in taking part? I am keen to get some sports personalities. I wrote to Steve Davis's (the snooker player) agent yesterday (fingers crossed!).

I would require all participants to attend six three hour sittings 'IDEALLY'. If you could not manage that many I would take some photos of you and use those for reference in your absence.

My plan is to go for a Greek theme and have everyone dressed in togas, lion cloths, sandals etc. (Would you have any objections to dressing up?). Behind you all I will paint a Greek temple with lots of classical columns etc. and you would each be holding a giant carrot (approx. 3ft long) as in 'carrot-tops'. These will be constructed of papier mache and quite light to hold. I would want to portray you all in a defiant, almost threatening mood, as if you are about to attack the viewer with your carrot.

From the sessions I plan to get individual portraits of each of you and a group portrait plus photos and interviews on 'life as a redhead'. I have now spoken to Hodder Headline and Collins, both of whom are interested in the idea of the book. This would be published in January 2000 to coincide with the opening of the exhibition 'REDHEADS AT THE REAR END OF THE MILLENNIUM'.

I have also had a meeting with Statics Ltd. with a view to 'Redhead' merchandise; Calendars, diaries, mugs etc. using my paintings. 10% of all proceeds will go to the retired taxi drivers fund (a very worthy charity).

You expressed some concern over the sitting for long periods (as have others). You are welcome to stand if you like, or recline. It is important you are comfortable.

Please let me know if you can take part, starting in April!?

I look forward to hearing from you again. Thanks for your phone number. I suffer from tinnitus and avoid phones at all costs. Cheers!

Yours sincerely,

Ocar Wendlows

BBC News

23 April.

Oscar Leadlow,
London SW13 0AA.

Dear Oscar,

Thanks for your letters & my apologies for the delay in replying — but I think not — not a project for me — but good luck with it.

Kind regards,

Nicholas Witchell

Nicholas Serota (Director)
The Tate Gallery of British Art,
Millbank,
London SW1P 4RG   19th January 1999

Dear Nicholas Serota,

I am a London Cab Driver of some 23 years standing but to be honest it has never
FULFILLED me in the 'SATISFACTION' sense. I was always 'yearning' to do
something creative and two years ago I started painting evening classes run by
Richmond Council. I took to it like a 'duck to water' and 'haven't looked back'.
My speciality is portraits of celebrities from the worlds of TV, film, the media, etc.
using magazine and newspaper photos for reference. I have been positively
CHURNING them out in the past couple of years and now have over eighty,
ENOUGH FOR AN EXHIBITION! (That's where you come in!)

I wondered if you might be interested in holding an exhibition of my work at the
Tate Gallery? I was thinking the show could be called 'BRITISH SUPERSTARS
OF THE ARTS AND MEDIA AND CULTURE AT THE REAR END OF
THE NINETIES'. People are always interested in celebrities so I'm sure it would
be of interest to the public. I would also like to be in the gallery every day to show
people around the exhibition and 'talk them through' the 'works', (I'm not one of
those aloof artists in an ivory tower). I could also deal with sales if anyone wanted
to buy one. DON'T GET ME WRONG, I'm not in it for the money. I am a
TRUE ARTIST. I would also be happy to donate a few of the paintings to your
permanent exhibition!

Fifty-two of the pictures I am VERY pleased with and about thirty are not so
good but if we were to mix up the good ones with the bad ones it would make an
assorted mixture of eighty, a 'respectable' number I am sure you will agree.

I hope you are interested and look forward to hearing from you ASAP. I can pop
in for a meeting anytime to discuss details.

Yours sincerely,

Oscar Wendlow

PS   Here are a few photos of some of my portraits. PLEASE RETURN
         THEM TO ME! (They cost a fortune these days!)

Tate Gallery
Millbank
London
SW1P 4RG
Tel: 0171-887 8000
Fax: 0171-887 8007

TateGallery

February 3, 1999

Oscar Wendlow
'Portrait Painter to the Stars'
 Cleveland Row
Barnes
London
SW13 0AA

Dear Mr Wendlow,

Thank you for your letter of the 19th January, proposing an exhibition of your painting at the Tate Gallery. Sir Nicholas has passed your letter on to us, and we have been able to consider your proposal.

I am afraid we could not offer you an exhibition at the Tate. Our exhibitions programme is fully committed and inevitably we have to turn down many proposals.

I am returning your photographs herewith. I wish you every success and thank you for your interest in the Tate.

Yours sincerely

Martin Myrone
Programme Curator
Tate Gallery of British Art

Trevor McDonald (Newscaster)
ITN News
200, Grays Inn Road
London WC1X 8XZ   4th December 1998

Dear Trevor McDonald,

My other 'alf and I are very sorry to hear that News at Ten is to be 'binned'. We have
watched it most nights for many years as have thousands of other people. We will also
miss you, Trevor. We are big fans of yours and almost feel as if you are an old
personal friend. We have always thought you strike just the right note of 'gravitas',
humour and personableness. We hear there is to be a later news at 11pm. Will you be
on that or are you retiring (to count your money, Ha, ha!)?

As you can see from my heading 'Portrait Painter to the Stars' my hobby is painting
pictures of celebrities. I have recently finished one of you which I am quite pleased
with (photo enclosed - which doesn't do it justice). I did most of it from memory but
on several occasions I worked on it 'live', studying you on News at Ten. I think it
makes you look a little younger but I'm sure you won't complain about that, Ha, ha!

Would you like to purchase it? It is 'oils' on board and measures about 3ft by 2ft. I
spent quite a lot of time on it so I was thinking of asking £350 for it. I could drop it off
to you personally. Perhaps I could even get to meet you! That would certainly be an
honour.

Please let me know ASAP if you are interested and we can discuss the details. I look
forward to hearing from you.

Best Wishes,

Oscar Wendlow

200 Gray's Inn Road
London WC1X 8XZ
Telephone 0171 833 3000
Facsimile 0171 430 4082

Mr Oscar Wendlow
 Cleveland Road
Barnes
London SW13 0AA

December 30, 1998

Dear Mr Wendlow

Thank you for your letter and the photograph of your painting of Trevor McDonald. It was most kind of you to think of sending it to him and he was delighted to receive it.

Trevor was also most happy to hear you enjoy watching News at Ten. As you know, this is soon to be replaced by our main news at the new time of 6.30pm, but it will still be presented by Trevor. We hope you manage to continue to watch.

Once again, thank you for writing. Your kindness was much appreciated.

Yours sincerely

Pauline Heard
PA to Trevor McDonald

Registered Office 200 Gray's Inn Road London WC1X 8XZ Registered Number 548648 England
Independent Television News Limited

Oscar Wendlow
'Portrait Painter To The Stars'
Cleveland Road, Barnes,
London SW13 0AA

The Rt. Hon Michael Heseltine MP
House of Commons
Westminster
London
SW1A 2PW   16th November 1998

Dear Mr Heseltine,

Last November I wrote to you asking if you would be interested in me painting your portrait. Unfortunately you were too busy at the time, NEVERTHELESS I am not one to give in easily, so I 'embarked' on a head and shoulders portrait of you, using newspaper photos for reference and I must say I am very pleased with the results. I definitely think it is one of my 'better' portraits (photo enclosed - which doesn't do it justice). In the picture I have put Maggie Thatcher in the background on your left to symbolise TORIES PAST and William Hague on your right to symbolise TORIES PRESENT. I have put a question mark over his head to indicate that his future is DOUBTFUL and a question mark over your head as if to say 'WILL HE EVER BECOME PARTY LEADER?' Then in the background I have put the sun rising to indicate a NEW DAWN if you WERE to become party leader and some doves to indicate HOPE because I HOPE that one day you WILL. And in the middle I have got YOU, smiling to yourself, thinking, 'Stuff the lot of them!' Ha, ha! and quietly making plans in your head.

I hope you like the painting and I would like to offer you the opportunity of 'purchasing' it. I know you have a stately home in Essex and I thought it might look rather tasty hung above a 'fireplace' surrounded by other paintings of your ancestors. It measures approx. 3ft by 2ft and in 'oils on board'. It took quite a long time to paint so I was thinking of charging £495 not including delivery costs. You might want to pop round and collect it personally - it would certainly be an honour to meet you.

Please let me know if you would like to buy it, then we can sort out the details.

You have been a bit quiet of late, Michael! I hope it won't be too long before you come BOUNCING BACK into the political limelight!

I look forward to hearing from you.

Yours sincerely,

Ocar Wendlow

HOUSE OF COMMONS
LONDON SW1A 0AA

27th November 1998

Oscar Wendlow Esq
  Cleveland Road
Barnes
London SW13 OAA

Dear Mr Wendlow,

Thank you for your letter of 16th November.

I regret that I am unwilling to purchase your painting.

Yours sincerely

The Rt Hon Michael R D Heseltine CH MP

Oscar Wendlow
'Portrait Painter To The Stars'
Cleveland Road, Barnes,
London SW13 0AA

Michael Buerk
Nine O'clock News
BBC TV Centre
Wood Lane
London W12 7RJ   10th February 1999

Dear Michael Buerk,

I am interested in becoming a 'newscaster' like yourself. For the past 23
years I have been a cab driver but am sick to death of it and am
DESPERATE for a career change before its TOO LATE. I paint (hence
my title, 'Portrait Painter to the Stars') and I write poetry, so I am not your
'common or garden' cab driver. I am someone who wants to MAKE A
MARK! Delivering the news to millions of people each night COULD BE
IT!

Would you be so kind as to drop me a line explaining how you got started
and could you answer the following questions on this sheet and return it?

Delete where applicable:-

1   Becoming a newscaster is:-
        easy/ very easy/ difficult/ very difficult

2   Newscasters are paid:-
        not very well/ well/ very well/ telephone numbers

Signed..(Michael Buerk)

Ta very much. I appreciate you taking the time and trouble. Please accept
the enclosed £5 as a small token of my gratitude.

Yours sincerely

Ocar Wendlow

British Broadcasting Corporation Room 1640 BBC News Centre Wood Lane London W12 7RJ Telephone 0181 624 9884 Fax 0181 624 9878

BBC News

Nine O'Clock News

11/2

Dear Oscar,

You'd hate it. Trust me, it's like cabbing without the variety, and the only people you get to meet are BBC people. Real life out there on the streets is much more interesting, even if it does throw up in the back of the cab on Saturday nights.

I started as a newspaper reporter, and was a television foreign correspondent for a long time — now that was a great job. Newscasting is a doddle, it's basically just a matter of reading out loud, any gabby cabby could do it — particularly with their famous grasp of current affairs. It's trying when things start to go wrong, but then your present job is, too, I dare say.

The money's not bad; more than the job is worth, to be frank, but don't tell the BBC or I'm out. Enough, anyway, to return your fiver. It was a kind thought, but if I kept it I would end up overtipping cabbies out of guilt, and it would cost me more in the long run —

All the best

Michael Buerk

137

HRH Prince Edward
Buckingham Palace
London SW1A 1AA   12th February 1999

Dear Prince Edward,

CONGRATULATIONS! I am chuffed to bits that you have finally taken my advice
and 'popped the question'. Well done! Sophie's a lovely girl and you won't regret it. I
must say it gives me immense satisfaction to know that my letters to yourself and
your mother (the Queen) have helped change the course of British history. Lets hope
it won't be too long before we hear the 'patter' of tiny royal feet! Although not before
nine months after the wedding, please! Ha, ha! Not that anyone's pretending you
don't already have a 'full' relationship. You're both young and healthy, its only
natural. I don't believe in 'waiting' BUT, having said that, an 'early' child would be
ill-advised and inevitably lead to whispers of 'shotgun'. I believe a royal birth
approximately 12 months after the wedding would be 'appropriate'. Lets face it,
Sophie's not getting any younger! You don't want to hang about.

Don't think marriage is a bowl of cherries, Edward BECAUSE IT AIN'T! At times its
bloody hard work. Separate beds was a big breakthrough for Joyce and me. She
always wanted to sleep under a mountain of quilts and blankets (cold blooded). I
preferred just a sheet (hot-blooded). Also, she is large so I kept rolling down into her
'dip'. I snore which disturbed her. She likes to eat in bed which caused a crumb
problem which annoyed me (its no joke waking up covered in crumbs) etc. etc. In the
end we decided on separate beds and 'haven't looked back'. If ever we feel the urge
to (hushed whisper) exercise our marital rights (end of hushed whisper. Ha, ha!) we
'do the business' on her bed then I return to mine and we both have a good nights kip.
I recommend it! (separate beds, not marital rights! Although I recommend that too.
Ha, ha!)

There was a lovely picture of you and Sophie on the cover of Hello! this week which
Joyce has stuck on the fridge, so you really feel like part of the family. Speaking of
which…. Any chance of a couple of invites to the wedding? Grovel, grovel. Ha, ha!
CONGRATULATIONS AGAIN and may we wish you a long and happy life
together. Don't hesitate to contact me if you need any further advice.

I look forward to hearing from you. Any chance of a signed photo?

Yours sincerely,

Oscar Wendlow

From: Lieutenant Colonel Sean O'Dwyer, LVO

BUCKINGHAM PALACE

16th February, 1999.

Dear Mr Wendlow,

Thank you for your letter of 12th February and I apologise that you have been put to the trouble of writing again. I am sure you will understand that it has taken some time to respond to the very large amount of mail which was received following the announcement of the engagement.

The Prince Edward has asked me to thank you very much indeed for your letter of 19th January, and for your extremely kind message of congratulations on his engagement to Miss Sophie Rhys-Jones.

His Royal Highness and Miss Rhys-Jones greatly appreciated your thought in writing and send their very best wishes.

Yours sincerely,

Sean O'Dwyer

Private Secretary to HRH The Prince Edward, CVO

Oscar Wendlow, Esq.

Oscar Wendlow
'Portrait Painter To The Stars'
Cleveland Road, Barnes,
London SW13 0AA

Libby Purves
Midweek
Room 6080
Broadcasting House
Portland Place
London W1A 1AA   10th February
1999

Dear Libby Purves,

I am a big fan of your radio show and YOU in particular. You have got a very warm,
friendly voice and (it has to be said) a much better sense of humour than most of your
guests. I am a cab driver 'for my sins' and I think my customers must think I'm a bit
'barking' when they hear me chuckling away at your 'asides' on a Wednesday
morning.

My hobby is painting portraits of celebrities hence the title 'Portrait Painter to the
Stars'. I usually work from newspaper and magazine photographs for reference. I
have been keen to paint you for some time, HOWEVER, I haven't been able to find a
picture of you ANYWHERE! For a long time I thought I would wait and HOPE that
your photo might appear in a newspaper. Then, one day I thought 'HANG ON A
MINUTE, OSCAR!' You are an 'ARTIST!' Use your IMAGINATION!

So that is what I have done and this is the result! I hope you like it. Could you let me
know if it is an accurate likeness and 'furthermore', would you be interested in
purchasing it? It measures 2ft by 3ft and is 'oils on board'. It took quite a long time to
paint so I was thinking of charging £350 for it, including delivery to Broadcasting
House (on a Wednesday morning of course, Ha, ha!)

Could you let me know ASAP if you are interested and thankyou again for your very
entertaining show. Long may it continue!

Yours in anticipation,

Oscar Wendlow

SUFFOLK

18th February 1999

Oscar Wendlow
  Cleveland Road
Barnes
London
SW13 0AA

Dear Oscar

Thank you for your letter. I am fascinated by your image of me but alas I don't have enough money to buy portraits of myself. Good luck with your artistic future which I suspect is going to be remarkable.

Yours sincerely

Libby Purves

Oscar Wendlow
'Portrait Painter To The Stars'
Cleveland Road, Barnes,
London SW13 0AA

Jeremy Clarkson
Top Gear
BBC Broadcasting Centre
Pebble Mill Road
Birmingham B5 7QQ

19th January 1999

Dear Jeremy Clarkson,

My other 'alf and I are BIG fans of Top Gear, NUTTY about anything to
do with 'motors' and HUGE fans of Formula One! Every time she sees a
picture of Damon Hill, Joyce practically has an orgasm. Ha, ha! Only joking!

Seriously though, Top Gear is a very entertaining prog. It's got everything;
technical spec! Humour! Music! And Personalities! Although I must admit
Joyce finds Quentin Wilson a bit 'smarmy'.

As you can see from my heading 'Portrait Painter to the Stars' I am a
budding artist (Sundays only). I 'specialise' in portraits of TV celebrities and
wondered if you might be interested in 'sitting' for me?

I imagine you leaning against the bonnet of a powerful sportscar holding a
spanner in one hand to indicate that you are a 'hands-on' petrol-head who
isn't afraid of getting his hands dirty. In your other hand you would be
holding a thick wad of money and looking at it with a funny expression, as
if to say 'shall I buy it or not?' Ha, ha! So the picture has a little sort of
'story' to it; Jeremy Clarkson in a dilemma! What do you think? Would you
be interested in taking part in this idea?

If there is anything about your appearance you don't like I could change it
in my picture. For example, I could make you shorter if you wished! Or
more handsome! Whatever!! I like my sitters to feel happy with the results.
Then the picture could be included in my next exhibition. I hope you are
interested in this idea and could find the time for half a dozen three-hour
'sittings'.

I look forward to hearing from you and wish you all the best. Keep up the
good work!

Yours sincerely,

Ocar Wendlow

British Broadcasting Corporation Pebble Mill Road Birmingham B5 7QQ Telephone 0121 432 8888 Fax 0121 432 8634

B B C Production

BBC Birmingham
Network Production Department

Oscar Wendlow Esq
  Cleveland Road
Barnes
London
SW13 0AA

22nd February 1999

Dear Mr Wendlow

Thank you for your letter addressed to Jeremy Clarkson. He is away filming at the moment, hence my reply.

It was very kind of you to offer to paint Jeremy but I am afraid he has neither the time nor the inclination to be painted at the moment.

Thank you again for asking him and for your kind words about Top Gear - Jeremy has stopped working on the programme now but is keeping up his motoring writing in the TG Mag, also the Sunday Times and the Sun.

Best wishes.

Yours sincerely

Francie Clarkson
(Jeremy's wife)

Oscar Wendlow
'Portrait Painter To The Stars'
Cleveland Road, Barnes,
London SW13 0AA

David Davies
FA Executive Director
16 Lancaster Gate
London W2 3LW   19th January 1999

Dear David Davies,

In recent weeks we have witnessed some appalling behaviour in premiership games and something has GOT TO BE DONE! As usual it is a few players bringing the whole game into disrepute with their highly dangerous tackles and fouls. And every time they do it they risk ending the career of their 'victim' through injury. IT HAS GOT TO STOP!

I would like to suggest a radical new system of punishment for these so-called 'sportsmen' which I believe would have immediate results. I call it punishment stripping or PS for short, and it goes like this; If a player commits a foul he has to remove his boots and play the rest of the game in his socks. If he commits another offence he has to remove his socks and play in his bare feet. Another and he removes his shorts, etc. etc. Of course the logical conclusion to this system is that a persistent offender would end up playing stark naked. SO BE IT! It might make the game a bit more interesting for the ladies, Ha, ha! But seriously, David, humiliation is an excellent deterrent. What do you think? Would you be prepared to put this idea to the FA board? I look forward to hearing your thoughts.

Yours sincerely,

Oscar Wendlow

Our Ref: MS/CHMN/991

26 February 1999

Mr O Wendlow
  Cleveland Road
Barnes
London
SW13 0AA

**THE FOOTBALL
ASSOCIATION**

PATRON
Her Majesty The Queen
PRESIDENT
H.R.H. The Duke of Kent

16 Lancaster Gate
London W2 3LW

Direct Tel:
Direct Fax:

Dear Mr Wendlow

Please accept our apologies for the delay in replying to your letter concerning your proposed alterations to the laws of the game.

Each year the Laws of Association Football are studied and amended by the International Football Association Board.

Your idea is certainly a novel one and has been noted.

Thank you for taking the trouble to write.

Yours sincerely

For the Executive Director

The Football Association Limited   Telephone 0171 402 7151   Facsimile 0171 402 0486
Registered Office 16 Lancaster Gate London W2 3LW   Incorporated in London Registration Number 77797

Oscar Wendlow
'Portrait Painter To The Stars'
Cleveland Road, Barnes,
London SW13 0AA

Jenny Tongue MP
House of Commons
Westminster
London SW1A 2PW   10th February 1999

Dear Jenny Tongue,

As a resident of Barnes I feel I must bring this 'condoms floating down the Thames' situation to your attention. My other 'alf and I are keen walkers and one of our favourites is along the river towpath to Putney. HOWEVER!, our strolls are becoming increasingly spoiled by the sight of all the rubbish floating in the water and the most disgusting 'constituent' of that rubbish is CONDOMS! Joyce and I were so amazed by the quantity that yesterday we stood in the same spot for half an hour and counted them. In that time FOURTEEN went past (one of them black). WHERE DO THEY COME FROM?! I find it hard to believe that people are 'having sex' on the river bank (IN THIS WEATHER!) and chucking them in. This leads me to conclude that they must be coming from HOUSEBOATS! These crafts are situated at Chelsea, Hammersmith, Chiswick, Kew, Brentford, Richmond, Twickenham and onwards upriver.

Clearly these people have no respect for the waterway they inhabit, indulge in sexual intercourse then toss their used condoms out of their portholes willy-nilly. They don't even tie knots in them which in my day was 'de rigeur'. This situation CANNOT be allowed to continue!

I suggest 'CONDOM WATCH', a team of plainclothes inspectors who could keep watch on houseboats at night with heat-sensitive binoculars and cameras. As soon as a window is opened and a condom (which would still be warm) is thrown out the heat-sensitive equipment could pick it up and photographic evidence produced in court. You could also send letters to all houseboat-dwellers threatening them with legal action if they are caught tossing their condoms overboard.

Let me know what you think. Something has got to be done to stamp out this FOUL, DISGUSTING and UNHYGIENIC littering of 'Old Father Thames'. I hope you agree and look forward to hearing your 'thoughts'.

Yours sincerely,

Ocar Wendlow

DR JENNY TONGE MP

HOUSE OF COMMONS

LONDON SW1A 0AA

March 3 1999

Mr Oscar Wendlow
 Cleveland Road
Barnes
London SW13 0AA

Dear Mr Wendlow,

Thank you for your letters of February 10 and March 1. I am sorry you have not had an earlier reply.

I keep being told by Thames Water and the Environment Agency how much cleaner the Thames now is and how efficient the purification system now is. I can't confess to seeing the problems you spot while I walk along the riverbank at Kew, but perhaps I am not looking hard enough!

Your suggestion that it is solely the Houseboats responsible for the problems is an interesting, but I think it might be a bit unfair to blame the debris totally on them.

I do however shortly have a meeting with the Environment Agency and I will raise your concerns with them.

I return the £5 you sent.

Yours sincerely,

pp: **Jenny Tonge (Dr.)**
Member of Parliament
for Richmond Park
ENC.

1

147

Oscar Wendlow
'Portrait Painter To The Stars'
Cleveland Road, Barnes,
London SW13 0AA

Mr. Paolo Galli
Italian Ambassador
Italian Embassy
14, 3 Kings Yard
London W1Y 2EH   1st October 1998

Dear Sir,

I am greatly concerned about the erosion of the British national character and you
'Italians' are largely to blame. LET'S FACE IT, ten years ago nobody in this country
knew what a cappuccino was or an expresso or café latte for that matter. WE ALL
DRANK TEA! and were perfectly happy thank you very much!

The same goes for pizzas. The first time I heard the word I thought it was a firework.
We didn't know what they were and we didn't miss them. Now they are
EVERYWHERE; Pizza Hut, Pizza Express, Domino's Pizzas, Bellini's Pizzas. How
many pie and mash shops do you see in the average High St? NONE!

I am very upset about this gradual 'Italianisation' of everything. Don't get me wrong,
I AM NOT A RACIST! I love the Italians. The way you shout and wave your arms
about is marvellous, and the Godfather is my favourite film. I simply believe that
countries should retain their individual characters. How would you like it if we filled
Rome with fish and chip shops and branches of Dixons?

I feel you should take steps to limit this tidal wave before we British lose our identity
altogether. Basta! Basta! (Stop, stop).

Something has got to be done. Please let me know your intentions.

Yours sincerely,

Ocar Wendlow

cc Tony Blair
cc Peter Mandleson
cc Chris Smith

The Italian Ambassador

Italian Embassy
4 Grosvenor Square,
London W1H 9SA

2 March, 1999

With reference to your letter dated 25 February, 1999 which was addressed to the Ambassador, I am returning, herewith enclosed, the £5 you sent.

The Ambassador has no comment to make on the contents of your letter.

Stefano Dejak
First Secretary

Mr. Oscar Wendlow
    Cleveland Road
Barnes
London SW13 OAA

Oscar Wendlow
'Portrait Painter To The Stars'
Cleveland Road, Barnes.
London SW13 0AA

Mr Latit Mansingh,
Indian High Commissioner
India House
Aldwych
London WC2 B4NA   2nd March 1999

Dear Mr Mansingh,

I read with ALARM in the newspaper the other day that there are now three times
more Indian restaurants in the UK than fish and chip shops! DON'T GET ME
WRONG! I am NOT a racist, but I AM concerned about the gradual erosion of the
British national character. How would you like it if we opened a branch of Dixons in
every street in Bombay?

I would like to suggest therefore that for the next few years at least, you impose some
restrictions on the business practices of your people and insist that they only open
Fish and Chip or Jellied Eel or Devonshire Cream Tea shops to restore the balance
and bring back a bit of national pride. What do you think?

I look forward to hearing from you.

Yours sincerely,

Ocar Wendlow

£5 enclosed for your admin. costs.

S.K. Mandal
Minister(Political)

भारत का हाई कमीशन
लन्दन

THE HIGH COMMISSION OF INDIA,

.... DEPARTMENT

INDIA HOUSE,
ALDWYCH,
LONDON WC2B 4NA

TELEPHONE: 0171-836 8484 EXT...............
TELEGRAMS: HICOMIND, LONDON W.C.2
TELEX: 267166 HCI LDN
FAX: 44 0171-836 4331

NO. Lon/MIN(POL)/1/MISC/98   March 15, 1999.

Dear Mr. Wendlaw,

        Please refer to your letter of March 2, 1999
addressed to the High Commissioner of India. I am taking the
liberty in responding on his behalf.

2.   I am delighted to know that you are not a racist. The idea
did not cross our mind. I appreciate your concern but I am sure
that you will admit that we have to role in defining the palatal
preferences of the British people who were, are and will remain
the supreme judge.

3.   I share with you your dream of having every street in
Bombay, or for that matter, any other city in India, having
shops full of computers and other high-tech items, many of which
may originate from U.K.

4.   Meanwhile, I am returning the £5/- note as you may
need it.

                                    Yours sincerely,

                                    (S.K. Mandal)

Mr. Oscar Wendlow
'Partrait Painter To The Stars'
   Cleveland Road, Barnes,
London SW13 0AA

Oscar Wendlow
'Portrait Painter To The Stars'
Cleveland Road, Barnes,
London SW13 0AA

Hubbard Casting
1, Old Compton St.
London W1V 5PH   4th February 1999

Dear Mr Hubbard,

I am interested in becoming a famous actor. Could you offer me any
advice on how to go about this and could we get together for a
'brainstorming' session? I am 53 years of age and don't have any acting
'experience' as such but am VERY KEEN. I gather there are usually
more parts for 'mature' actors than youngsters, is this true? I wrote to
Barbara Windsor and she suggested 'acting lessons' but I am not so
sure. I believe I am a 'natural' and working as a taxi driver for 23 years
teaches you a LOT about human nature! I also paint portraits of
celebrities in my spare time, so I am 'all round artistic'.

Could we get together for a meeting to talk things through and form a
career plan? Also, how does one 'break' into Hollywood?

I look a bit like Danny De Vito only taller and thinner and less bald.

I look forward to hearing from you. I am VERY DETERMINED!
This isn't just some flash in the pan!

Yours in anticipation,

Ocar Wendlow

P.S. £10.00 enclosed to cover your admin costs.

HUBBARD CASTING

Oscar Wendlow
  Cleveland Road
Barnes
London
SW13 0AA

23rd March 1999

Dear Mr Wendlow,

Thank you very much for the £10.00, but it is not custom & practice to receive money.

We are truly not available for general meets at the moment.

Most of our work involves trained actors.

Perhaps you should contact British Actors Equity and they can give you some advice.

Yours sincerely

Ros Hubbard.

Ros Hubbard.

13 Colville Place, London, W1P 1HN, Tel: 0171 636 9991, Fax: 0171 636 7117

Oscar Wendlow
'Portrait Painter To The Stars'
Cleveland Road, Barnes,
London SW13 0AA

Frank Dobson MP   27th January 1999
Secretary of State for Health
House of Commons
Westminster
London SW1A 2PW

Dear Frank Dobson,

I am not a labour voter! I am a life long TRUE BLUE TORY
ROYALIST! However, I must admit that I feel sorry for you. You have
a very difficult job to do, running the National Health Service, and this
is an especially difficult time of year.

Part of the problem is too many people going to their G.P.'s too often
and wasting their time. For these people going to the doctor is almost a
weekly event, like buying the groceries. And they cost the taxpayer
BILLIONS!

This is why I am writing to you! I have a small 'complaint' and I do not
want to waste my doctor's time with it. It is a small rash under my left
armpit. It is red in colour and feels dry and 'flaky' although it is not
sore. I stopped using deodorant for a week but that didn't make any
difference. I have also tried applying Vaseline 'to no avail'. I wonder if
you or anyone in your department might have any idea what it could be
and how best to treat it. Could you ask around? I'm sure you can
understand that I am reluctant to waste my G.P.s precious time with
something so small.

I look forward to hearing from you.

Yours sincerely,

Oscar Wendlow

Richmond House 79 Whitehall London SW1A 2NS Telephone 0171 210 3000
Direct line 0171 210

Mr Oscar Wendlow
  Cleveland Road
Barnes
London
SW13 0AA

Your Ref:
Our Ref:

9 March 1999

Dear Mr Wendlow

Thank you for your letter of 23 February to Frank Dobson.

I understand that you are reluctant to visit you GP with what you consider to be a small complaint. However your GP is there to deal with this sort of complaint as well as more serious conditions.

I am sure you will understand that the Secretary of State for Health is not in a position to make a postal diagnosis of anyone's medical conditions. I recommend you visit your GP who is in the best position to advise on your complaint.

I am returning your five pounds with this letter.

Yours sincerely

Jim Howard
Ministerial Correspondence Unit

09/03/99

IMPROVING THE HEALTH OF THE NATION

Oscar Wendlow
'Portrait Painter To The Stars'
Cleveland Road, Barnes,
London SW13 0AA

Andy Parfitt
Radio One Controller
Broadcasting House
Portland Place
London W1A 1AA   2nd March 1999

Dear Andy Parfitt,

I am writing to ask if you would consider playing my son Raoul's first 'single' on
Radio 1. I regret to say his band has the disgusting name of 'Vomit for Breakfast' and
the single is called 'Hairy Armpits' but they are actually a nice bunch of lads and the
song is quite catchy (they produced it themselves).

The reason I am asking this special favour is that Raoul has been through a difficult
time of late and he needs all the breaks he can get. He was recently 'chucked' by his
girlfriend, 'Gabby' after an incident in the car park of Sainsbury's Homebase,
Richmond in which he backed my car into a palette of bathroom tiles causing her
severe 'whiplash'. She has been in a neck-brace ever since.

No sooner had she chucked him than he discovered he had a mild form of a venereal
disease (NSU). This upset him because it meant that Gabby had been sleeping around
(surprise, surprise!) It annoyed me because I had been preaching 'safe sex' until I was
blue in the face (God knows what else he might have caught! It doesn't bear thinking
about!)

Then, in the same week he was asked to appear in an identity parade at Twickenham
Police Station to 'make up the numbers'. Guess what? HE WAS PICKED! One
minute he was being a good samaritan, helping the forces of law and order – the next
minute he was being questioned about a 'flashing' incident on the towpath at
Teddington.

Unfortunately his alibi in the flashing incident is wholly dependant on Gabby (he was
at her flat at the time) and she is refusing to vouch for him so he is now the PRIME
SUSPECT.

Fortunately he has had Vomit for Breakfast as a distraction throughout this horrible
ordeal and if they could play Hairy Armpits on Radio 1 it would be absolutely
brilliant and really cheer him up. PLEASE LET ME KNOW IF YOU CAN AS
SOON AS POSSIBLE then I will get Raoul to drop a tape into you personally.

Thank you very much for your co-operation and assistance.

Yours in eager anticipation,

Oscar Wendlow

British Broadcasting Corporation Yalding House 152/156 Great Portland Street London W1N 6AJ Telephone 0171 580 4468 Fax 0171 765 1439

BBC Broadcast

From Controller, Radio 1

Mr O Wendlow
   Cleveland Road
Barnes
London
SW13 0AA

9 March, 1999

Dear Oscar,

Thank you for your letter dated 2nd March 1999 regarding your son's first single.

All of our music is selected by the Producers and the Playlist committee who select singles to be played on Radio 1 on their musical merit. If, and when, your son has a record to listen to he is very welcome to send it to the Head of Music Policy, Jeff Smith.

Thank you for your £10 to cover our administration fees, but I have decided to donate it to comic relief.

Yours sincerely,

PP *Cordelia P. Harries*

Andy Parfitt

Oscar Wendlow
'Portrait Painter To The Stars'
Cleveland Road, Barnes,
London SW13 0AA

Michael Parkinson
Parkinson
BBC TV Centre
Wood Lane
London W12 7RJ

5th March 1999

Dear Michael Parkinson,

Congratulations on an excellent new T.V. series. It's great to see you back after all these years and it's very encouraging to blokes like me to see that you are never too old to make a comeback!

I have been a cab driver for the past 23 years, but am SICK TO DEATH of it and am DESPERATE to do something else, something CREATIVE! Let's face it, Michael, we all want to make a mark in life. What's it going to say on my gravestone? "He drove a cab very well"? IT'S NOT ENOUGH, MICHAEL! I want to leave something behind me when I 'pass on'. It's alright for you, you've made your mark, you're a National Institution, you've ACCOMPLISHED something! You could die tomorrow and be happy! You're FULFILLED! and I'M NOT!.

That is why I am writing to you. Apart from driving a cab I also paint portraits of celebrities and I wondered if you might be interested in using them in your show? What I 'had in mind' was about fifty of my portraits as a 'backdrop' behind you and your guests on the show. The paintings would all be of famous old 'stars of yesteryear' who you have interviewed, then if you were telling an anecdote about one of them you could point to the relevant painting (I would provide you with a long white stick). Perhaps you could even talk about me a little bit and mention that the paintings are 'for sale'. Maybe you could have me on the show?! I'm quite a character and I've got plenty of anecdotes to tell,
a woman once left £2,400 in the back of my cab, for example!

I hope you are interested in my idea and very much look forward to hearing from you. I am enclosing £10 to cover your admin costs.

Yours in anticipation,

Ocar Wendlow

P.S. I am also enclosing seven photos of my celebrity portraits, including; Trevor McDonald, Cilla Black, Jeremy Paxman, William Hague, Angus Deayton, Michael Heseltine and Jeremy Clarkson. I hope you like them.

B B C Production

16th March 1999

Oscar Wendlow
   Cleveland Road
Barnes
London
SW13 OAA

Dear Mr Wendlow

Many thanks for your letter containing the kind words of praise for PARKINSON , which has been passed on to me.

Unfortunately, we are not going to be able to take you up on the offer to use your paintings as a backdrop for the set. We plan to carry on using the current set for a while and will not need a replacement, but thanks for the suggestion.

I have returned the £10 you enclosed for admin costs along with the seven photos of your celebrity portraits, which I think are brilliant - Trevor McDonald, Angus Deayton and Jeremy Paxman are my favourites, but they're all great.

I do hope you find success in your ambition to carry on doing something creative. The fact that you know that you <u>want</u> to be creative puts you ahead of the crowd already.

Sorry not to have been more encouragement, but the best of luck with everything you do in the future. Thanks once again for all your interest in PARKINSON.

Yours sincerely

DANNY DIGNAN
Producer, Parkinson